Julia Constantia Chase Washburn

Genealogical Notes of the Washburn Family

with a brief sketch of the family in England, containing a full record of the descendants of Israel Washburn of Raynham, 1755-1841

Julia Constantia Chase Washburn

Genealogical Notes of the Washburn Family
with a brief sketch of the family in England, containing a full record of the descendants of Israel Washburn of Raynham, 1755-1841

ISBN/EAN: 9783337091361

Printed in Europe, USA, Canada, Australia, Japan

Cover: Foto ©ninafisch / pixelio.de

More available books at **www.hansebooks.com**

OF THE

WASHBURN FAMILY,

WITH A

BRIEF SKETCH OF THE FAMILY IN ENGLAND.

CONTAINING A FULL RECORD OF THE

DESCENDANTS OF ISRAEL WASHBURN

OF RAYNHAM,

1755-1841.

ARRANGED BY MRS. JULIA CHASE WASHBURN.

1898.

Works Consulted.

Mitchell's "History of Bridgewater," 1840. Emory Washburn's "Judicial History of Massachusetts," 1840. "Two Hundredth Anniversary of Bridgewater," 1856. "Notes of Livermore," Israel Washburn, Jr. "In Memoriam," by family of I. Washburn, Jr. "An address on Henry Gratiot," by E. B. Washburne, 1884. Peach's "Notes and Records of the Washbourne Family," 1896. "Divine Poems" of Thomas Washbourne, D. D., 1654. With Memorial Introduction by Rev. A. B. Grosart, 1868. "Brief Notice of Lieut. Samuel Benjamin."

English authorities are given where quoted.

Thanks are also due the members of the Washburn family who have contributed to the value of this book by patiently answering the many questions which were asked them; and especially to those who in addition to this favor, kindly gave access to the material for the notes of the family in England.

J. C. W.

Livermore, November 1, 1898.

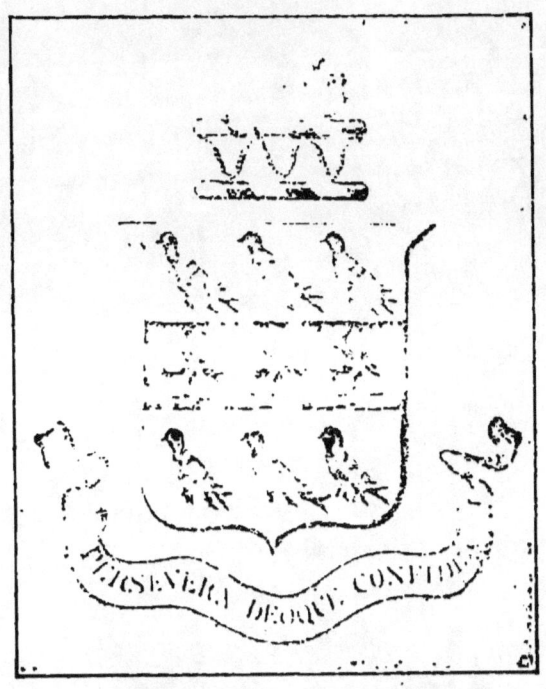

ARMS OF WASHBOURNE.

WASHBURN GENEALOGY.

NOTES OF THE WASHBOURNE FAMILY IN ENGLAND.

Grosart puts the date of the Washbourne family before the Norman Conquest (11th Century).

In Herald's College, London, Vol. I., page 54, is given: WASHBOURNE. A name of ancient Norman descent; the founder was knighted on the field of battle by William the Conqueror and endowed with the lands of Little Washbourne and Great Washbourne, Counties of Gloucester and Worcester.*

In his "Britannia" Camden says: Under these Bredon Hills southward you see two villages named Washbourne, whence came the surname to a very ancient and worshipful Family in this tract.

Nash in his history of Worcestershire says: Little Washbourne, anciently Wassebourne, (which means literally Water brook) is sometimes called Knight's Washbourne from the knightly character of the Washbournes, who took their surname from hence; for men generally have their names from towns and not towns from men.† He also says the family of Washbourne

---

*Grosart says while Great Washbourne is in the borders of Gloucestershire, Little Washbourne is in Worcestershire, but not distant.

†Nash's History of Worcestershire, Vol. II., p. 263.

were Lords of Stanford, and that Sir Roger de Washbourne held in Stanford what his father, Sir John de Washbourne, formerly held. Stanford passed to John Solway in his marriage with Isolde Washbourne about 1400 A. D.

Grayerbrook in "Heraldry of Worcestershire," Vol. II., p. 609, says: Washborne—of Washborne, Wichenford and Stanford: This ancient family was seated at Little Washborne in Overbury before the reign of Edward III. Roger de Washborne, living about the reign of Edward III., had two sons both named John. The elder having no issue, was succeeded by his grand nephew, John Washborne of Washborne and Stanford, the son of Peter Washborne who was the son of John, the younger son of Roger de Washborne.

John Washborne was twice married; by his first wife Joan, daughter and heiress of Sir John Musard, he had one daughter— Isolde—who married John Solway and carried with her the Stanford Estates. He married 2d Margerey Poher (or Power), daughter of Lord John Poher, by whom he inherited large estates at Wichenford in 1397. After his marriage with Margerey Power, John Washborne lived at Wichenford (and died there May 13, 1454. The Washborne family conti..... to live at Wichenford for six generations. The following names appear in the line:

NORMAN, High Sheriff, married Elizabeth Kynaston. Son of John Washbourne and Margerey Power.

JOHN of Wichenford, son of Norman.

ANTHONY, born 1513, married Anne Rede.

JOHN, Twice High Sheriff of Worcestershire, Justice of Peace 60 years. Married, 1st, Mary Savage, 2d, Elenor Lygon; died 1633, aged 85. Tomb to himself and his father, Anthony, in Wickenford church.

JOHN, married Alice, daughter of Henry Robinson. Citizen of London. Died 1615, aged 48.

WILLIAM, married Lettice, daughter of Lord Lyttleton. Died, 1622.

JOHN, born 1620. A prisoner at battle of Worcester. Compounded for his estate with Parliament (1651) for £797 10s. Married Elizabeth Child.

Col. John Washborne, born 1620, was a distinguished Royalist in the time of the Rebellion. He joined King Charles II. at Worcester, Aug. 26, 1651, "with forty horse." At the battle of Worcester, which Cromwell called "a crowning mercy," he was taken prisoner and compounded with Parliament for his estate by paying £797 10s—but the author of Magna Britannia tells us "He was even with them paying them more than once in another metal." He was fined by Charles I., for not taking the Order of Knighthood, £35. He married Elizabeth Child. His daughter Mary married Sherrington Talbot, from whom the present Earl of Talbot is descended. She died March 30, 1661, at Stourton Castle and is buried at Kenvir, Co. Stafford.

The direct male line of Washbornes of Wichenford expired in the person of William Washborne who sold Wichenford in 1712 to Mr. Skynner, and afterward resided at Pytchley in Northamptonshire. By his marriage with Hester, daughter of

Sir John Ernle, he had one daughter, Elizabeth, who married Frances Money-Kyrle, Esq., whose descendant, Audley Money-Kyrle, has recently repaired the Washborne tombs in Wichenford Church.

THE OLD MANOR-HOUSE AT WICHENFORD.

Wichenford Court was one of the largest mansions in Worcestershire with moat, drawbridge, etc. It stands near Wichenford church, about six miles northwest of the city of Worcester and about twenty miles from Great Washbourne and Little Washbourne (Stanford). Wichenford parish contains 2,672 acres.

In Edward III.'s time a family of the name of Poher was seated at Wichenford. From them it passed to the Washbornes through the marriage of John Washborne with Margerey Poher (commonly called Power) 1397. The male line failing, it was sold from the family in 1712. Since then it has passed through many hands and has recently been purchased by Admiral Daniel Britten, who lives in and is owner of the adjoining parish of Kenswick (1897).

The interior of the house appears to be older than the external brick casing, and one of the rooms on the ground floor is still an object of interest to the antiquary, with an enriched frieze and cornice running round it, and contains an elaborate Jacobæan chimney-piece in oak.

The fireplace is flanked with pilasters, and above it are two panels between grotesque caryatids. The dexter panel contains a shield with the Washbourne arms, mantling, and crest with burning flax. In the other is a rebus, some kind of a plant issuing out of a tun, referring perhaps to the wife's maiden name.

In the frieze are grotesque lions' masks; the whole being of rude but sumptuous character.*

Some of the fine old wainscoting was removed from Wichenford Court in 1895 and put up at Kenswick by Admiral Britten. Some Washbourne portraits, said to resemble American Washburns, are also to be found in the Kenswick mansion of Admiral Britten, which were removed from Wichenford Court.

It was in this old Washbourne Manor-house at Wichenford that one of the Bourbon Princes was confined and is said to have been put to death by Lady Washbourne in the absence of her husband, when Owen Glendower was encamped on Woodbury Hill in the reign of Henry IV.

*W. Niven's " Illustrations of old Worcestershire Houses," p. 31.

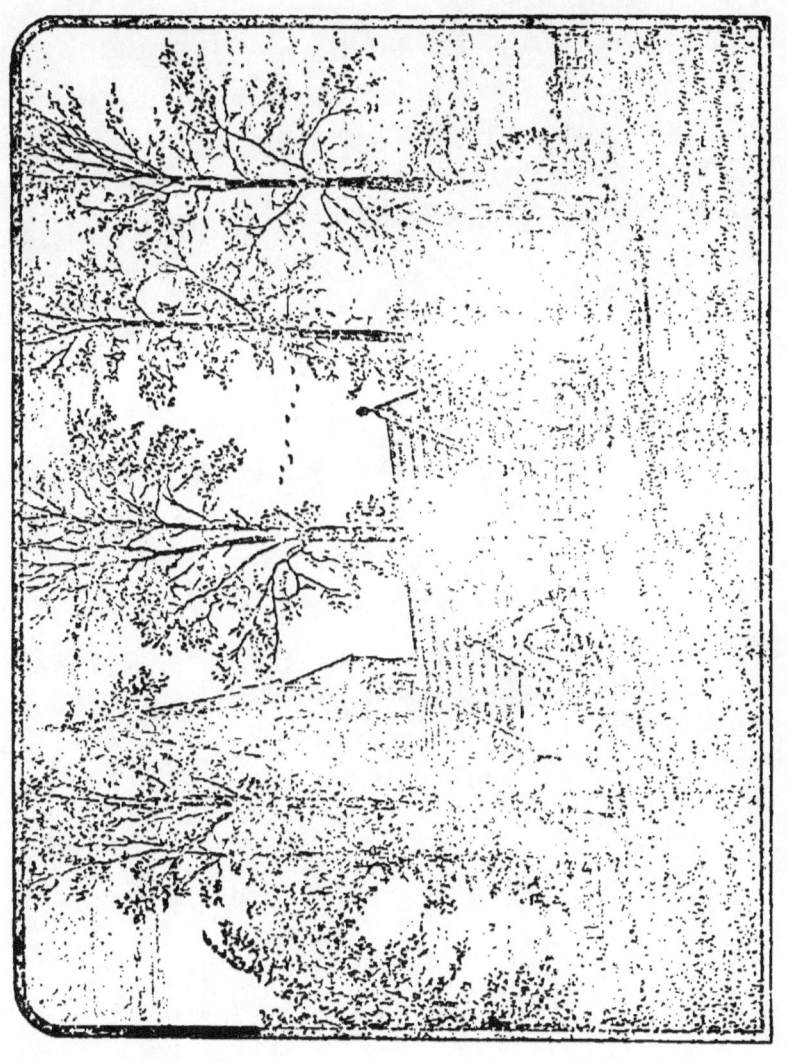

WICHENFORD CHURCH, IN WORCESTERSHIRE, ENGLAND.

OLD CHURCHES AND TOMBS.

Near the old Washborne Manor-house at Wichenford is the old parish church, built in 1262 and dedicated to Saint Lawrence. After extensive restoration in 1863 it was reopened for public service.

The oldest portion is the tower, which has duplicated buttresses set square at the angles and in each wall a small lancet light. The interior has a steep-pitched, open-timbered roof, a well-proportioned chancel arch and seats accommodating about two hundred worshipers.

In this church are two monuments of the Washbourne family, which were also restored in 1863 by William Money-Kyrle, Esq., of Homme House, Herefordshire, who is a descendant of the Washbournes, being a great-great-grandson of Elizabeth Washbourne of Wichenford, who was married to Frances Money-Kyrle, Esq., A. D. 1723.

One of these tombs was erected by John Washbourne (Sheriff). The original inscription is now gone; and instead of it, is a brass plate at the base of the tomb inscribed thus:

"This monument was erected by John Washbourne, Esq., in pious memory of his father, Anthony Washbourne, Esq., as also of himself and his two wives, the first Mary, daughter of Francis Savage of Elmley Castle, Esq., and the second, Elenor, daughter of Richard Lygon of Madresfield, Esq., descended from one of the co-heiresses of the Lord Beauchamp of Powick. The

said John Washbourne being at the time of this inscription (1632) of the age of 84 years." (He died in 1633.) On this tomb are effigies of John Washbourne and his son, probably, both armed except the head, at their feet a lion; and above these in niches in the wall are two gentlewomen kneeling, being portraitures of his two wives. Between them are Washbourne arms, being Argent, on a fess between six Martletts Gules, three quatrefoils of the first. This tomb is on the north side of the chancel.

In the southwest corner of the church near the font is another monument. The original inscription is gone; but on the wall below the Washbourne arms, quartered with the arms of Power, is a brass plate thus inscribed:

"In memory of John Washborne, Esq., grandson of Anthony Washborne, Esq., and son of John Washborne, Esq., (and also of his wife and children) who departed this life 25th Sep. 1615 aged 48." On the north side of this monument kneel two sons and a daughter.

W. Habbington, who first took these transcriptions, adds that "He (John Washborne, Sheriff of Worcestershire) was the best continual housekeeper and the best beloved Gentleman in the County."

He was the father of seven sons and six daughters.

Nash speaks of two other Washborne tombs which were in Wichenford Church in 1640, now gone, one inscribed "Here lie the bodies of John Washbourne Esquire and Margerey Power his wife." He died May 13, 1454. The other, "Here lies John Washbourne Esq., son of Norman Washbourne Esq." With Washborne and Power arms.

In Pytchley Church, Northamptonshire, within the rails of the altar is a stone inscribed:

"William Washbourne Esq; was buried xith day of August, 1702." Upon four freestones on the ground in the chancel:

I. "Here lieth the body of John Washbourne, Gent., who was taken out of this world the 16th of Jan. 1685."

II. "Mrs. Elizabeth Gray, daughter of William Washbourne Esq., was buried the 26th day of March 1692."

III. "Mrs. Elizabeth Washbourne, buried Feb. 7th 1700."

IV. "Here lies Richard Washbourne, sixth son of William Washbourne, Esq., who departed this life 23d December, 1704.

Mrs. Ann Washbourne, 1757. Widow. Hester Soums, daughter of W. Washbourne, aged 89."

"On Sep. 8, 1743, there died in St. James Street, Westminster, Early Washbourne Esq., and his 'corps' was brought with great pomp and solemnity to Northampton and lay in State that night at the Red Lion Hotel and the next morning was carried to Pytchley and interred."

Elizabeth Washborne, dau. of Thomas Washborne of Stanford, mar. John Pakington, ancestor of Lord Hampton, is buried at Hampton Lovett.

Elenor Washbourne, who married 1st Sir Richard Scrope and 2d Sir John Wyndham, is buried in the choir of the Austin Friars in Norwich.

In the records of Durham Cathedral can be seen the names of Wilhelmes de Wasseborne and Johannes de Wasseborne— 1360 A. D.

In the Cathedral at Gloucester there is a tomb under the floor of the Ladies' Chapel. On the slab that covers the tomb

is the Washbourne coat of arms (three cinquefoils). This is the tomb of Thomas Washbourne, D. D., who was prebend of the Cathedral forty-four years. He took his degrees at Balliol College, Oxford, A. B., 1625; A. M., 1628 and D. D., 1636.

Grosart says "Thomas Washbourne, D. D., was born at Wychenford Court 1607, and was son of John Washbourne and Elenor Lygon, if I do not misread the somewhat intricate roll of the Washbournes." He died May 6, 1687, in the 80th year of his age.

Like his kinsman, Col. John Washbourne, Thomas Washbourne was a zealous Royalist, in the time of the Rebellion, and preached a famous sermon called " The Repairer of the Breach " in Gloucester Cathedral, May 29, 1661, " being the anniversary of His Majesty Charles II.'s birthday and happy entrance into His Emperial City of London."

He also published in 1654 a small volume of "Divine Poems." These poems were reprinted for private circulation in the Fuller Worthies Library, with a Memorial Introduction and Notes by Rev. Alexander B. Grosart in 1868, and several copies have been brought to America by different members of the Washburn family.

The following stanzas are from one of the " Divine Poems " of Thomas Washbourne, D. D., called

Angels Our Guardians.

" How dear to God is man
That He His mercy should enlarge
To this poor span,
And thus to charge
His Angels to keep every limb
Of him.

Old Churches and Tombs.

" Such are his strict commands
To them, that they are bound to bear
Him in their hands,
Secure from fear
Of dashing but his foot upon
A stone."

The Slab that covers the tomb of Thomas Washbourne has a long Latin inscription, to which he requested this humble addition, " Chief of Sinners and least of God's Servants."

In the same Chapel is a tomb to the brother of Thomas Washbourne, inscribed: " Sacred to the memory of the Rev. William Washbourne, M. A., a most worthy Prebend of Gloucester Cathedral, and fellow and ornament of Oriel* College Oxford. He gave up his spirit on his bended knees Nov. 28, 1675, in the 60th year of his age."

John Washbourne, M. A., Rector of Holt, Co. Worcester, obit. Aug. 11, 1689, aged 48. Buried at Holt.

Eliza Washbourn died at 27 and is buried in the Unitarian Chapel at Gloucester. In this Chapel and adjacent burial ground there are many interesting memorials to members of the Washbourne family.

---

*One said merrily he wished he had a sinecure for he thought his parts lay much that way—It was one Washborne of Oriel.—Ward's diary of 1648.

GLOUCESTER WASHBOURNS.

The defeat of the King at the battle of Worcester and the subsequent forfeiture of the estates of Washbourn and Wichenford drove Daniel Washbourn to seek his bread in Gloucester, in which city his brothers Thomas and William held brebendal stalls in the Cathedral. Here his descendants continue to live, and published in 1896 " Notes and Records of the Washbourne Family."

COAT OF ARMS.

The Washbornes entered their arms in the Herald's College, London, A. D., 1633, and their arms and pedigree A. D. 1569 and 1634.

Burke's General Armory gives:

"WASHBOURNE.—County of Worcester; a family of knightly degree, previous to time of Edward III. Direct male line ceased with William Washbourne of Wichenford and Pytchley, Esq. (1726) who married Hester, daughter of Sir John Ernle of Wrentham, Co. Wilts, knight, who left an only daughter, Elizabeth Washbourne, who married Francis Money of Willingborough, Esq.

ARMS: Argent on a fess between six Martletts gules, three cinquefoils of the field.

CREST: On a wreath a coil of flax argent, surmounted with another wreath argent and gules, thereon flames of fire proper."

MOTTO: "Persevera Deoque Confide."—[Given at Herald's College Vol. 1 p. 54.]

(Martletts indicate 4th son.)

An earlier arms differs from this in having three quatrefoils instead of three cinquefoils; with motto "Purificatus non Consumptus."

THE NAME.

The name of Washburn is derived from two words. Wash, which implies the swift current of a stream, and bourn or burne is simply a brook or stream.*

The name is variously spelled in the early records, and in this book the spelling of the original documents is followed.

The name is still spelled Washbourne in England, but in America the simpler Washburn is almost universal. The family of Hon. Elihu B. Washburne use the final "e."

The earliest form of the name seems to be de Wassebourne.

---

*Edgar.—"Come o'er the bourn, Bessy, to me;"
Fool.—"Her boat hath a leak
    And she must not speak
Why she dare not come over to thee."
—*King Lear.*

EVESHAM BRANCH OF WASHBOURNE FAMILY.

Burke says the Evesham and Wichenford branches of the Washbourne family are from the same stock, both coming from the Difford and Great Washbourne family. Evesham is in the County of Worcester and about twenty miles from Wichenford.

The earliest mention of the Washbourne family at Evesham is in the reigns of Henry III. and Edward I. when they occupied the Evesham Abbey lands. [1216-1307.]

John Washbourne was one of the first twelve Burgesses, constituted by the Charter of Evesham, granted by King James 1. in the 3d year of his reign (1605).

John Washborne was the first Secretary of the Plymouth Council in England, and was succeeded by William Burgess in 1628. Whether the last mentioned John Washborne was from Evesham and whether he ever came to America are matters on which genealogists differ.

PLYMOUTH COUNCIL
AND
JOHN WASHBORNE ITS SECRETARY.

In 1606 King James gave a sweeping grant of the Continent of America between latitudes 34 and 45 to two Companies: the Southern part to the London Co., and the Northern to the Plymouth Company. March 4 (15 new style) 1628 King Charles I. conferred a charter to the Plymouth Co., under which a corporation was created by the name of "The Governor and Company of the Massachusetts Bay in New England." It was of the Council of these companies, " Plymouth " and "Massachusetts Bay," that John Washborne was Secretary till 1628, when he resigned and William Burgess took his place and came to America with Gov. Winthrop, 1630.

The following letter relating to John Washborne, Secretary, is of great interest to the antiquarian:

TAUNTON, Mass., Dec. 1, 1898.

Mrs. Julia Chase Washburn, North Livermore, Me.:

Madame—

I have just returned from Boston where I spent a half hour in the office of the Secretary of the Commonwealth, in the examination of the first record book of the BAY COLONY. This first record was made by "Jno Washborne" and I enclose the record of the vote appointing him (John) 1st Secretary; I have signed his name as it is written on the records and I enclose the copy just as written, spelling, etc., the same as in the book.

Sincerely Yours,
GEORGE A. WASHBURN.

Plymouth Council

The 9 Marche 1628

This day John Washborne is entertayned for Secretary for one whole yere to enter the courts to keepe the Companys accounts to make warrants for all Moneys to bee brought in or payed out and to geeve nottice at every meeting of such as are backward in payment of there subscriptions also for all purcession to bee made reddy, to call uppon such as have ye chardge whereof w'by the shippes nowe bound ffor Newe England May be dispatched by the 25 of this month at ffurdest; his sallery ffor this yeere is to...... he in the prenisses & the office of a secretary to pf (orme) ffaithfull dilligent & tr (eue) (i) ndevurs whervnto he doeth fulley & agree.

Jn̄o. Washborne

JOHN WASHBORNE.

John Washborne of Evesham was the first of record who came to America. The pros and cons of his being identical with the John Washborne who was connected with the Massachusetts Bay Co. in London are given below:

Judge Mitchell in History of Bridgewater says: "John Washburn* was the first Sec'y of the Plymouth Council in England. Whether he had any connection with the family in America is not known."

Ex-Gov. Emory Washburn in "The Judicial History of Massachusetts," says: "The first Secretary of the Company (Plymouth) was John Washburn, but as he never came to America we have little to do with his history." (1840.) But in 1856 this same Mr. Washburn, at the 2d Centennial Celebration of Bridgewater, said, "As I glance at the present Congress and see a name there three times repeated I shall hardly be charged with indelicacy if I recall the part which the first who bore it (in this country) took, after his traditionary connection with the Massachusetts Colony had ceased, as one of the Duxbury men, in the event we are now celebrating."

In a foot-note on same page is the following: "John Washburn is believed to have been the first Sec'y of the Massachusetts Colony."

*Judge Mitchell says the name is spelled in the early records of Massachusetts, Washborne, Washburne, Washborn and Washburn, but he uses the last spelling *only* in his History of Bridgewater.

John Washborne

In the Biography of Gov. Israel Washburn of Portland, printed by his family, he is there spoken of as a descendant of John Washburn of Evesham, "who is understood to have been the Sec'y of the Plymouth Council." In Appleton's Cyclopedia of American Biography Vol. VI. p. 370, E. B. Washburne and C. C. Washburn are spoken of as descendants of John Washburn, first Sec'y of Council of Plymouth in England, who came to Duxbury, Mass., 1631.

The investigation is still going on. Mr. L. P. Godell of Fort Worth, Texas, who designs to bring out an exhaustive history of the Washburn family in England and America, says, " I must candidly say I am not to-day settled upon the identity of the two John Washburns, but I am studying the matter thoroughly."

Col. George A. Washburn of Taunton, Mass., says: "I would like to be one of a number to raise a fund to settle this question whether 'Our' John was the Sec'y in 1828 in England, but I have *no doubt* of it."

FIRST WASHBURNS IN AMERICA.

Judge Nahum Mitchell in History of Bridgewater, Mass., says: "John Washburn was early in Duxbury, Mass. He had an action in court against Edward Doten 1632, is named in the assessment of taxes 1633 and purchased Edward Bompasse's place, called 'Eagle's Nest,' 1634. He and his sons, John and Philip, were included in those able to bear arms, 1643, and his name is among the first freemen of Duxbury. John Washburn and his son John were two of the fifty-four original proprietors of the town of Bridgewater, Mass., 1645. They bought it of Massasoit, sachem of the country of Poconocket for the following consideration:

7 Coats, a yard and a half to a coat,	
9 Hatchets,	Signed,
8 Hoes,	Miles Standish
20 Knives,	Samuel Nash
4 Moose-skins,	Constant Southworth."
10½ yards of cotton.	

First Generation in America.

FIRST GENERATION OF WASHBURNS IN AMERICA.

1. JOHN WASHBURN was born at Evesham, County of Worcester, England, and came to Duxbury probably in 1631. His wife, Margery (aged 49), and two sons joined him there in 1635, coming on the ship Elizabeth. They went to live at Bridgewater about 1665 and he died there before 1670.

Children of John and Margery Washburn:

I. JOHN, born in Evesham, England, about 1621. +
II. Philip, born in Evesham, England, about 1624. Died unmarried.

SECOND GENERATION IN AMERICA.

2. JOHN WASHBURN, son of John[1] and Margery Washburn, was born in Evesham, County of Worcester, England, about 1621. He came to Duxbury with his mother and brother Philip, aged 11, 1635, on the ship Elizabeth.

He married at Duxbury, 1645, Elizabeth Mitchell, whose father, Experience Mitchell, was one of the forefathers of the Colony, was with the pilgrims at Leyden, and came to Plymouth on the third ship, the "Anne," 1623. Children of John[2] and Elizabeth Washburn:

I. JOHN[3], married Rebeckah Lapham.
II. THOMAS[3], married, 1st, Abigail Leonard, 2d, Deliverance Packard.
III. JOSEPH[3],* married Hannah Latham, granddaughter of Mary Chilton.
IV. SAMUEL[3], born 1651; married Deborah Packard.
V. JONATHAN[3], married Mary Vaughn of Middleboro', Mass.
VI. BENJAMIN[3], died in Phipps' expedition against Canada.
VII. MARY[3], married Samuel Kinsley, 1694. Kingsley
VIII. ELIZABETH[3], married, 1st, James Howard; 2d, Edward Sealey.
IX. JANE[3], married William Orcutt, Jr.
X. JAMES[3], married Mary Bowden, 1693.
XI. SARAH[3], married John Ames, 1697.

John[2] Washburn died at Bridgewater before 1690.

EX-GOVERNOR EMORY WASHBURN.

*Ex-Gov. EMORY WASHBURN was descended from Joseph[3] Washburn. He was born at Leicester, Mass., 1800. He graduated at Williams College, 1817. He was in the General Court of Mass., 1826 and 1827, and in the Senate 1841 and 1842. He was appointed Judge of Court of Common Pleas 1844, resigned 1847. He was elected Gov. of the Commonwealth in 1853. He accepted the Bussey professorship of law in Harvard University in 1856 and filled the position till his death, March 18, 1877. He died at Cambridge. The line of Emory Washburn is as follows:

John[1] Washburn and Margery ————.
John[2] Washburn and Elizabeth Mitchell.
Joseph[3] Washburn and Hannah Latham, granddaughter of Mary Chilton.
Joseph[4] Washburn and Hannah Johnson.
Seth[5] Washburn and Mary Harrod.
Joseph[6] Washburn and Ruth Davis.
Emory[7] Washburn and Marianne C. Giles.

---

*Rev. Alfred Washburn, an Episcopal clergyman and son of Emory Washburn, died at Cambridge in 1896. A daughter, Mrs. Batchelder, is living at Cambridge.

THIRD GENERATION OF WASHBURNS IN AMERICA.

3. SAMUEL, son of John,[2] was called "Sergeant Washburn." He was born at Duxbury, Mass., 1651.

He married Deborah Packard. Her father, Samuel Packard, came from Windham near Hingham, England, on the ship "Delight of Ipswitch," and settled at Hingham, Mass., 1638. He afterward lived at West Bridgewater, Mass.

Children of Samuel and Deborah Washburn:

I. SAMUEL[4] born 1678; married Abigail ———.
II. NOAH[4], born 1682; married Elizabeth Shaw, 1710.
III. ISRAEL[4], born 1684; married Waitstill Sumner, 1708.
IV. NEHEMIAH[4], born 1686; married Jane Howard, 1713.
V. BENJAMIN[4], born ———; married Joanna (or Susanna) Orcutt.
VI. HANNAH[4], born ———; married John Keith, 1711.

Samuel[3] died at Bridgewater, Mass., 1720, aged 69. He was the ancestor of the Maine family of Washburns. The next seven in the line bore the name of Israel Washburn. To the last two was added the name of Henry—making the name Israel Henry Washburn.

FOURTH GENERATION OF WASHBURNS IN AMERICA.

4. Israel Washburn, son of Sergeant Samuel[3] and Deborah Packard Washburn, was born at Bridgewater, Mass., 1684.

He married Waitstill Sumner in 1708.

Children of same: All born in Bridgewater.

I. Sarah[5], born 1709; married Ephraim Keith, 1732.
II. Deborah[5], born 1712; married, 1st, John Ripley, 2d, Nathaniel Bolton.
III. Seth[5], born 1714.
IV. Israel[5], born August 11, 1718; married, 1st, Leah Fobes, 2d, Hannah Keith.

Israel[4] Washburn died at Bridgewater 1719. He was the last of this line of Washburns who lived in Bridgewater. His son, Israel[5] Washburn, settled in Raynham and his descendants continue to live there.

The widow of Israel[4] Washburn married Ebenezer Pratt, 1720.

FIFTH GENERATION OF WASHBURNS IN AMERICA.

5. ISRAEL WASHBURN, son of Israel[4] and Waitstill Sumner Washburn, was born at Bridgewater, Mass., Aug. 11, 1718. In 1740 he married Leah Fobes, who was born at Bridgewater March 27, 1720. She was the daughter of Joshua and Abigail Dunbar Fobes, and a descendant of John Fobes who was one of the original proprietors of Bridgewater. John Fobes married Constant Mitchell, an aunt of the wife of John[2] Washburn.

Rev. Perez Fobes, D.D. (Harvard, 1762), whose "Call" to preach at Raynham is given on page 32, and who was the settled pastor there from 1766 till his death, 1812, was her relative.

Israel[5] Washburn settled at Raynham, Mass., shortly after his marriage and all his children were born there. He died at Raynham Jan. 21, 1796. His wife, Leah Fobes Washburn, died there Dec. 9, 1789. He married, 2d, Hannah Keith of Bridgewater, who died the same month as himself.*

Israel[5] Washburn was elected March 4, 1776, a member of the Committee of Correspondence, Inspection and Safety for the town of Raynham. He was also Captain of the military Co., —the train band—of Raynham, Nov. 9, 1774 (and previously). Said Co. was one of the companies of the 3d Regiment of Bristol County.†

*History of Bristol Co., Mass. Page 709.

†For anecdote of Israel[5] Washburn see page 79.

He also served a short time in the Revolutionary army. Record: Israel Washburn, Sr., appears as Sergeant on Muster and pay rolls of Capt. John Shaw's Co. Col. Abiel Mitchell's Regt. for service at Rhode Island on the alarm of Aug. 2, 1778, discharged, Aug. 10, 1778. Service eight days. Commanded by James Williams in Gen. Godfrey's Brigade. Marched to Tiverton by order of Council. [Office of Sec'y of Mass. Vol. III. p. 131.]

The military was entirely reorganized in 1776—the four Regiments of Bristol Co. formed the Bristol Co. Brigade and George Godfrey was made Brigadier Gen'l Commanding. The following letter from Gen. Godfrey is kindly furnished by the Sec'y of the Old Colony Historical Soc'y.

LETTER OF GEN. GODFREY.

"Sir:—

The several foot companies of Taunton have been assisting in forming three companies of *Minuit* Men, as recommended by the provincial Congress, and I suppose it would be necessary that your two companies should Raise one by the name of *Minuit* Company, and if you should Like the method Taken at Taunton I suppose there will be no difficulty in coming in to the same way. I shall be for such a plan. Should be obliged to you to Let Capt. Israel Washburn know of my Desire.

I am, etc., etc.,

GEORGE GREGORY."

Taunton, feb. 20 1775.

To this the Sec'y adds, "Now, it is remarkable that a man like Israel Washburn, so noted as to be in command of a Co. in Raynham, in 1774, and so prominent and respected in his town as to be one of the Committee of Inspection and Correspondence

in 1776, should in 1778 perform service as a Sergeant in Capt. John Shaw's Co. at the alarm at Rhode Island. But the solution of the whole matter is—that every able-bodied person probably between 16 and 65 was obliged to bear arms at that time, and rank and estate did not count."

The following letter in the handwriting of Israel Washburn[5], is in the possession of his great-granddaughter, Mrs. Ellen Washburn Smith of Auburn, Maine.

"The Church of Christ in Raynham, To ye Ch.h of Christ in e.
Sendeth Greeting.
Whereas some time Since, God in his Ever adorable providence was Pleased to remove by Death our Rev'd Pastor, Mr. John Wales. Since which time we have been Destitute of ye Settled administration of the ordinances of ye Gospel of Christ among us. Having Sought ye Lord by prayer and for Sometime Past ymproved Mr. Peres Forbes to preach with us, and having Gained a good degree of Satisfaction Touching his ability and accomplishments, The Brethren and Congregation here Have United in Giving ye Said Mr. Forbes a Call to settle among us in the work of ye Gospel ministry and he having been inclined and Disposed to accept our Call we have mutually agreed upon the ordination—These are therefore Beloved & Honored Brethren to Give you an ynvitation To Send your Elders and Messengers to joyne with and assist us in the Solemn Ordination of the Said Mr. Forbes to the Pastoral Cares of ye Chh and congregation in this place. And after asking your prayers for us that we may be Sharers yn ye Blessings of the New & Everlasting Covenant we are to Subscribe our Selves your Sincere well wishers in the Blessings of ye Gospel.
(Signed)
ISRAEL WASHBURN.

Raynham, Nov. 1766.

Children of Israel[5] and Leah Fobes Washburn.

Their first three children died at an early age and near together, "leaving naked walls" as the father sadly said. The order of birth of the others is not definitely known, but it is thought the oldest was

IV. LEAH[6]. She married Jason Fobes of Bridgewater about 1770.

V. ISRAEL[6], born 1755, married Abiah King of Raynham, 1783.

VI. NEHEMIAH[6]. Married Polly Presho, lived and died in Raynham. His children were Oliver Cromwell[7], Nehemiah[7], Davis[7], Calvin, Lysander[7], Isaac[7], John Marshall[7], Mahala, Thirza, Fanny and Cordana.

Davis Washburn married Deborah Williams of Taunton and had four sons, born in Livermore, Me., namely: George, John, James and Nehemiah. The widow of Davis Washburn married William Henry Brettun of Livermore. Mahala[7] married Elijah Gushee of Raynham. Thirza married Clothier Knapp; (their daughter Cleora Knapp married Jefferson Coolidge of Livermore.) Fanny married Horatio Leonard.

VII. SETH[6] was a physician. He married Lydia Shaw, lived and died in Raynham. His Children were Philo[7], Benjamin Franklin[7], Amelia[7], Julia[7], Deborah[7], Flora[7] and Stella[7]. Amelia married J. L. James of Chicago. Julia married Isaac Leonard (brother of Payton Randolph Leonard). Deborah married Rev. James Thompson, a Unitarian minister, and Stella married Rev. Samuel Dean, a Unitarian minister of Scituate.

VIII. OLIVER[6] married Sally Lascom and lived and died in Raynham. His children were Otis[7], Caleb Strong[7], Rhoda[7], Mary[7], Charlotte[7], Sarah and Pamelia. Mary married William Snow of Raynham. Charlotte married Rev. George Leonard, Unitarian minister of Marshfield.

IX. OLIVE[6] married Reuben Andrews of Raynham. His son, Orrin Andrews, married Prudence Reed of Livermore.

X. PRUDENCE married —— Keith ——.

SIXTH GENERATION OF WASHBURNS IN AMERICA.

6. Israel, son of Israel[5] and Leah Fobes Washburn, was born in Raynham, Mass., Jan. 30, 1755.

He was a soldier in the war of the Revolution and the following is an official abstract of a part* of his service:

"Commonwealth of Massachusetts, Office of the Secretary:—
· Revolutionary War Service of Israel Washburn, Jr.

Israel Washburn, Jr., appears with rank of private on Lexington Alarm roll, of James Williams, Jr.'s, Company, which marched on the alarm of April 19th, 1775, from Taunton to Roxbury. Residence, Taunton (?) (Raynham.)†

Israel[5] Washburn was a tall, large-framed man, and in the prime of life very straight and strong, but much bowed in age. He served in the General Court of Massachusetts several years and was a member of the Convention that adopted the first constitution of the Commonwealth.

He talked but little, and it is said that in all his legislative experience he made but one speech. On one occasion a member having made a speech that greatly pleased him he arose and said: "I like what that man said, because—*I do like it.*"

Israel[6] Washburn married in 1783 Abiah King, daughter of Benjamin and Deliverance Eddy King. She was born in Raynham June 29, 1762.

*The record of Israel Washburn, Jr.'s further service in the Revolution does not appear—but as some of the early records were lost, that was doubtless of the number.

†Raynham was a part of Taunton till 1731.

Sixth Generation in America

Children of same: All born in Raynham.

I. Israel[7], born in Raynham, Mass., Nov. 18, 1784. Died at Livermore, Me., Sept. 1, 1876. ÷ 7
II. Molly[7], born Nov. 14, 1786. Died in Raynham, Aug. 7, 1874.
III. Sidney[7], born Nov. 14, 1788. Died at Bowdoinham, Me., Jan. 1, 1811.
IV. Benjamin[7], born Feb. 10, 1791. Died at Greenfield, Ohio, July 1, 1830.
V. Reuel[7], born May 21, 1793. Died at Livermore, Me., March 4, 1878.
VI. Elihu[7], born July 22, 1795. Died at Raynham, March 28, 1812.
VII. Philander[7], born June 29, 1799. Died at Raynham, Dec. 8, 1815.
VIII. Eli King[7], born July 22, 1802. Died at Raynham, July 28, 1852.
IX. Lydia King[7], born Feb. 24, 1805. Died at Livermore, May 9, 1865.
X. Cornelia[7], born Jan. 7, 1807. Died at Raynham, Dec. 22, 1842.

Israel[6] died at Raynham Jan. 8, 1841, aged 86. His wife, Abiah King Washburn, died May 25, 1842, aged 80.

"THE NORLANDS."

There have been three different houses on the site where "The Norlands" now stands.

The first was built and lived in by Dr. Cyrus Hamlin. The older Hamlin children were born in it, but Vice-President Hannibal Hamlin was born at Paris, Me., 1809. Dr. Hamlin sold the place to Artemas Leonard when he moved to Paris, and Mr. Leonard sold it to Israel[7] Washburn in 1809.

It was a large, square, two-story house; and in it all the children of Israel[7] and Martha Benjamin Washburn were born. It is told that all were carried *up stairs* before being carried *down* for a good omen.

In 1843 this house was replaced by a modern white cottage with green blinds, and a French window opening from the sitting room to the piazza. In 1867 this cottage was enlarged by the addition of a two-story wing on the north, making a very picturesque house, but before it was entirely finished it took fire and burned. The present mansion, "The Norlands," was built immediately after the burning of the other, which was called "Boyscroft," 1868.

"The Norlands"

"When the long dun wolds are ribbed with snow,
And loud the Norland whirlwinds blow."*
—*Tennyson. (Oriana.)*

Poem.

Written in "The Norlands" Journal Aug. 13, 1883,
By Miss Ellen Hamlin Butler,
(A niece of Mrs. Hannibal Hamlin.)

I.

Far up among the hills of Maine,
  Whose rugged summits rise
From dimpling lake and smiling plain
  To meet the distant skies,—
Where Summer, like a blissful dream
  Steals in among the pines
And wreathes the rocky-bedded stream
  With dainty tinted vines;—

II.

Where Winter holds a royal reign,
  And winds his mighty horn
Above a world without a stain
  On every flashing morn;
"The Norlands" lie serenely fair,
  As, in the magic seas,
Encircled by enchanted air
  Lay the Hesperides.

III.

And here, apart from worldly strife,
  From sordid gain and greed,

---

*Origin of the name "The Norlands" given to the Washburn homestead, 1868.

A noble band awoke to life,
  Of lofty thought and deed.
They drank the inspiration taught
  On every granite hill;
They learned the lessons interwrought
  With every singing rill.

IV.

A Nation's sons were they, who saw
  What statesmen only see;
They laid their hands upon her law
  And shaped her destiny.
Tread gently, reverently, when
  Ye come upon this sod;
Here sprang a race of giant men,
  The handiwork of God.

FAMILY OF ISRAEL⁷ WASHBURN.

7. Israel Washburn, son of Israel⁶ and Abiah King Washburn, was born in Raynham, Mass., Nov. 18, 1784.

He came to Maine in 1806. He taught school a year or more in Lincoln County, Maine, and engaged for a time in shipbuilding with Barzillai White, at White's Landing, now Richmond, on the Kennebec River.

The following letter was written by him to his sister Molly Washburn at Raynham on his 23d birthday.

NEWCASTLE, MAINE, Nov. 18, 1807.

"I had the pleasure of receiving those letters which you were generously pleased to forward by the hand of Mr. Gray; which I received on the 30th of Sept. They were to me a sumptuous repast indeed, to have so direct and pleasant intelligence from friends and relatives so near cannot but excite in any mind the most pleasant sensations.

When I received your letters I was engaged in teaching school in the town of Woolwich; the time that I wrote you of keeping was three months; but their intentions were that I should board from house to house, which I did not wish to do; so they had money sufficient for two months only. My term was then nearly half expired and not knowing where I should next be engaged, I neglected writing till I had completed there and commenced in another school.

You wished to know the state of my school, my amusements, society, etc. As to my school, it consisted of young and old as the generality do, very backward in the attainments of learning and almost without spirit for improvement.

However, I was well treated. The man with whom I boarded was a farmer of large property who lives extremely well, and I should have enjoyed myself well had I had books for my amusement; these I had not, and my leisure hours I employed at farming.

The school I am now engaged in appears more promising. It consists of about 14 scholars, who according to their age, opportunities, etc., are superior to those in general; are very docile and tractable. I am very well pleased with my situation. It is on the banks of the pleasant Damariscotta, which is navigable for vessels of any burthen as far as I am from the sea. There is considerable business done here in the navigation line. There are arrivals every few days from Europe or the West Indies.

Capt. James Little, the man with whom I am boarding, is a man of good sense, considerably improved by information. His family are principally girls, who are grown up, are very amiable and handsome, with minds improved by reading and good company.

I am some distance from meeting; we have, however, a respectable minister and good society. I attended last Sunday and was well entertained.

I cannot trouble you with a long narration of books I have read since I last wrote. While I was in Woolwich I read little from want of books. Since I have been here I have read "The Female Review, or Life and Adventures of Deborah Sampson." It is very pleasing from the novelty of the character and the heroism she displayed. I don't admire the style, it being, I think, too bombastic and appears too studied.

I have also read Moore's "Monitor," which is a collection of pieces from the best of authors, especially from the Spectator. Such writings cannot I think be too much studied.

I am now in a situation to procure more books and I hope in my next to be able to inform you of them and make observa-

tions on their contents. The autumn has been uncommonly pleasant, till this day which is a violent snow-storm. I have enjoyed my health, by the blessing of Providence, since I left home without interruption. I have no special news to state. Peace and quietness I believe reign without interruption. You will on the receipt of this forward one to me as soon as possible and I shall not I hope neglect writing so long a time again. I send my love and respect to my parents and brothers. I am much obliged to Sidney for his communications and hope he will not discontinue them. Elihu has my thanks for his pleasing paper. You will please to direct your letters to Wiscasset, as I shall be frequently there. Mr. Gray and Mr. White are in good health you may inform their friends......I have nothing further at present but to request you to overlook all imperfections and subscribe myself   Your brother,

Israel Washburn Jr.

Israel⁷ Washburn came to Livermore, Me., in 1809. He bought the farm, store and goods belonging to Artemas Leonard and began business as a trader, which he continued till 1829. He lived on this place, which was later called "The Norlands," the remainder of his life.

In the early years of his residence in Livermore Mr. Washburn was much in town office; and he was a Representative to the General Court of Massachusetts (before the separation of Maine, 1820) in 1815, 1816, 1818 and 1819.

He was blind the last years of his life. His eyes were operated upon for cataract without success in 1859. After which

time some member of his family read to him regularly the daily news in which he never lost his interest.

He was a man of great cheerfulness of disposition, and rivalled Lincoln as a story-teller.

His memory was wonderful in accuracy and tenacity. He could name every member of Congress and tell his District at the time he had three sons in Congress.

The following fitting tribute to Israel Washburn is found in the journal of his son, Elihu B. Washburne, written in the besieged city of Paris, during the Franco-German war, when he was Minister to France:

"Friday evening, Nov. 18, 61st day of the Siege.

This is the eighty-sixth birthday of my father. All hail to the glorious, great-headed, great-hearted noble old man! In truth the noblest Roman of them all.

How intelligent, how kind, how genial, how hospitable, how true.

Yet when in the course of nature a kind Providence shall call him hence, I would have the hand of filial affection only trace this simple inscription on his monument: 'He was a kind father and an honest man.'"

This wish was carried out and one can read this inscription to-day upon his monument in Waters' Hill Cemetery overlooking "The Norlands."

MARTHA BENJAMIN, WIFE OF ISRAEL WASHBURN[1].

Martha (or Patty) Benjamin was born at Livermore, Oct. 4, 1792. She was the daughter of Lieut. Samuel and Tabitha Livermore Benjamin.

Martha Benjamin was one of Nature's Noblewomen.

After her death Mrs. J. H. Hanson, in the "Star and Covenant" of Chicago, said of her: "Mrs. Washburn's life was one of great purity and excellence; her character was one of marked womanly force, impressing itself by a quiet yet irresistible influence on all who knew her. A genuine Christian wife and mother, reverenced wherever known. Her house was ever the minister's home."

Rev. George Bates, once her pastor at Livermore, said: "As a wife and mother, Mrs. Washburn had few superiors in our land. Upon her children she has left the impress of her character and they will rise up and call her blessed."

Her portrait, painted by her grandson, Cadwallader L. Washburn, has recently been hung in the Orphans' Home, dedicated to her memory, in Minneapolis, Minn.

LIEUT. SAMUEL BENJAMIN, FATHER OF MARTHA BENJAMIN WASHBURN.

Hon. Israel Washburn, Jr., in "Notes of Livermore," gives the following:

"Samuel Benjamin was born in Watertown in the Province of Massachusetts Bay, Feb. 5, 1753.

He was a descendant, in the 5th generation, from John Benjamin, who arrived on the ship "Lion," 1632, and was a "proprietor" of Cambridge and Watertown, Mass.

Gov. Winthrop speaks of him as "Mr. Benjamin," and he had the largest homestall at Watertown. He died there June 14, 1645.

Samuel Benjamin, on the breaking out of the Revolutionary War, joined the Company of Capt. Daniel Whitney, of which he was sergeant.

He was at the battle of Lexington, Apr. 19, 1775, also at Bunker Hill, at Monmouth, at Yorktown, and many other battles.

His whole term of service was seven years, three months and twenty-one days.

"It is doubtful if any man of the Revolution was in more battles or saw more or harder service."

Lieut. Samuel Benjamin married Jan. 16, 1782, Tabitha Livermore of Waltham, Mass., where she was born, June 27, 1757.

She was a sister of Nathaniel Livermore of Cambridge and a relative of Dea. Elijah Livermore for whom the town of Livermore was named, their common ancestor being Samuel

Lieut. Samuel Benjamin

Livermore of Watertown, who died Dec. 5, 1690. The wife of Rev. Rufus Stebbins, D. D., of Cambridge (who died 1898) was of the same family of Livermores.

In the fall of 1782 Lieut. Benjamin made a trip to the "District of Maine," and on the 10th of October he bought of Dea. Livermore 120 acres of land on the west side of the Androscoggin River, bordering on the South Side of "Long Pond." The same land is now owned (1898) by Elias Morse. The house is not standing.

In 1797 Mr. Benjamin bought a farm on the east side of the Androscoggin, where he died April 14, 1824.

His wife died at East Livermore June 20, 1837.

Samuel Benjamin was the fourth settler with a family in the town of Livermore.

BENJAMIN GENEALOGY.

Children of Samuel and Tabitha Livermore Benjamin:

I. BILLY, the second male child born in Livermore. Born 1785. Died 1849. Married Phœbe Wellington.
II. SAMUEL, born 1786. Died 1871. Married Olivia Metcalf.
III. NATHANIEL, born 1788. Died 1867. Married Betsey Chase.
IV. BETSEY, born 1790. Died 1860. Married Samuel Morison.
V. POLLY, born Oct. 4, 1792. Died 1865. Married Samuel Ames.
VI. PATTY or MARTHA, born Oct. 4, 1792. Died May 6, 1861. Married ISRAEL WASHBURN.
VII. DAVID, born 1794. Died 1883. Married Catherine Stanwood (who died 1882).
VIII. CHARLES, born 1795. Died 1834. Married Lucy Chase.
IX. ELISHA, born 1797. Died 1852 at New Orleans.
X. RUTH, born 1799. Died 1869. Married Jonathan Lovejoy.

The marriage of Israel Washburn and Martha Benjamin took place March 26, 1812, at Livermore (now East Livermore.)

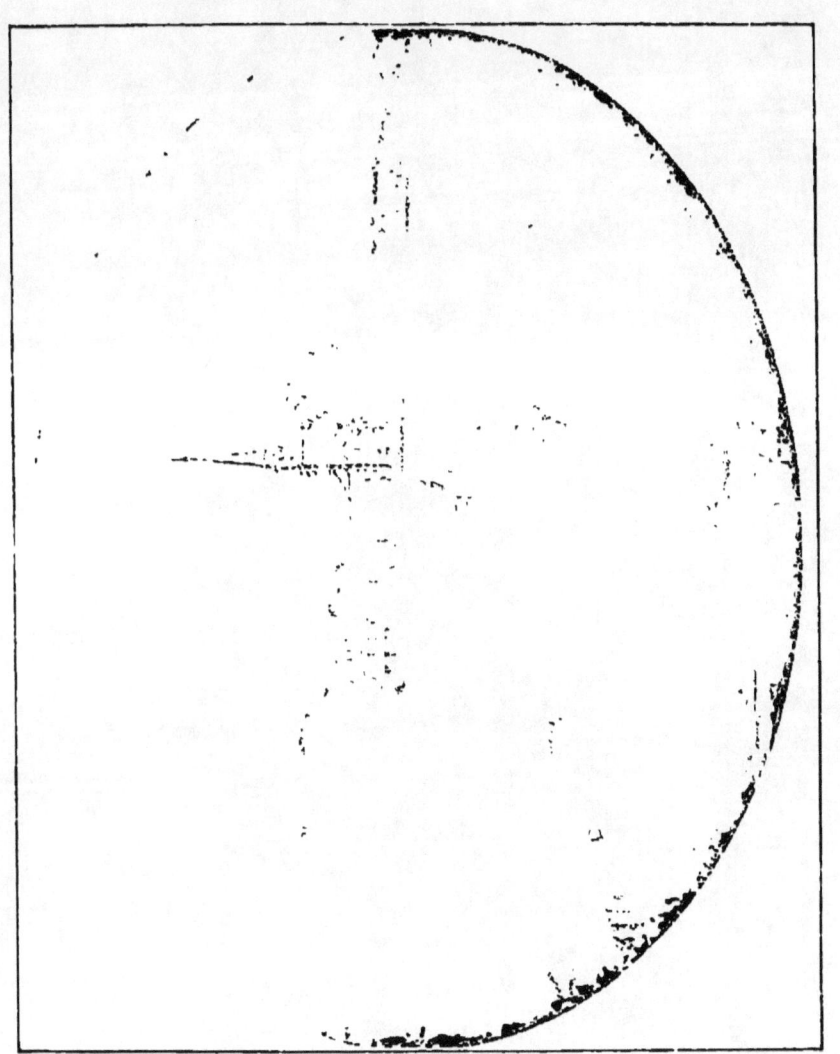

"THE NORLANDS," LIVERMORE, ME.

Notes of Washburn Genealogy

CHILDREN OF ISRAEL[7] AND MARTHA BENJAMIN WASHBURN.

All born at Livermore.

I. ISRAEL[8], born June 6, 1813. Died at Philadelphia, Pa., May 12, 1883, aged 69 years, 10 mos. 29 days.
II. ALGERNON SIDNEY[8], born Nov. 29, 1814. Died at Hallowell, Me., Sept. 29, 1879, aged 64 years 10 mos.
III. ELIHU BENJAMIN[8], born Sept. 23, 1816. Died at Chicago, Ill., Oct. 22, 1887, aged 71 years, 29 days.
IV. CADWALLADER COLDEN[8], born April 22, 1818. Died at Eureka Springs, Ark., May 14, 1882, aged 64 years, 22 days.
V. MARTHA BENJAMIN[8], born Feb. 6, 1820.
VI. CHARLES AMES[8], born March 16, 1822. Died at New York City, Jan. 26, 1889, aged 66 years 10 mos. 10 days.
VII. SAMUEL BENJAMIN[8], born Jan. 1, 1824. Died at Avon, New York, March 4, 1890, aged 66 years, 2 mos. 3 days.
VIII. MARY BENJAMIN[8], born Nov. 11, 1825. Died at Lyons, Iowa, March 15, 1867, aged 41 years, 4 mos. 4 days.
IX. WILLIAM ALLEN DREW[8], born Oct. 22, 1827. Died at Livermore, Nov. 28, 1828, aged 1 year, 1 mo. 6 days.
X. WILLIAM DREW[8], born Jan. 14, 1831.
XI. CAROLINE ANN[8], born Jan. 30, 1833.

Israel[7] Washburn died at Livermore, Sept. 1, 1876. Aged 91 years 9 mos. 13 days.

Martha Benjamin Washburn died at Livermore, May 6, 1861. Aged 68 years 7 mos. 2 days.

FAMILY OF ISRAEL WASHBURN, JR.

8. ISRAEL WASHBURN, Jr., son of Israel[7] and Martha Benjamin Washburn, was born at Livermore, June 6, 1813.

His education was obtained from the public schools and from private instruction in Latin and Greek from his uncle, Reuel Washburn, who was a graduate of Brown University.

With this uncle he read law and later with Hon. Theodore Brown of Vassalboro.

He was admitted to the bar and settled at Orono, Maine, October, 1834.

He was elected to the State Legislature in 1842. He was Representative, from the Bangor District, to the 32d, 33d, 34th, 35th and 36th Congresses; first as a Whig, and as a Republican after that party was formed in 1856.

In 1860 he was elected Governor of Maine as a Republican, and served two years, declining a re-election.

He was appointed by President Lincoln, Collector of the Port of Portland in 1863, after which time Portland was his home.

For many years he was President of the Board of Trustees of Tufts College, from which he had received the degree of Doctor of Laws. He devoted his last years to literature; his published works being a volume of "Notes on Livermore," an exhaustive paper on the Northeastern Boundary question, as well as various memoirs, addresses and lectures.

Tribute to Hon. Israel Washburn, Jr.

The following sonnet was published in the Bangor "Whig and Courier" during the exciting discussion in Congress on the Slavery question in 1854.

> "All hail to thee, thou Champion of our State!
>   Thou guardian of its interests in this hour
>   Of mad attempts to strengthen Slavery's power,
> And fix on Freedom's soil its curse and fate!
> Thou'rt not ashamed before the proud and great—
>   None greater than thyself—to utter forth
>   The free bold language of thy native North!
> A language taught by Nature's alphabet,
>   It's letters, mountains and the rushing streams,
> Broad bosomed lakes and forests unexplored,
>   The deafening thunder and the lightning's gleams,
> And all that tells of FREEDOM seen and heard,
>   This is thy language—thine, too, the reward!"
>   EDWARD M. FIELD.

8. Israel Washburn, Jr., married at Orono, Maine, Oct. 24, 1841, Mary Maud Webster, of whom there is the following notice in the Historical and Genealogical Register for April, 1874:

"Washburn, Mrs. Mary Maud, died in Minneapolis, Minn., June 30, 1873. She was the daughter of Col. Ebenezer and Mrs. Lucy (Dudley) Webster and was born July 24, 1824, in Orono, Me., where she was married Oct. 24, 1841 to Israel Washburn, Jr., since a member of Congress and Governor of Maine and now Collector of Customs for the district of Portland, Me.

She was a lineal descendant of Gov. Thomas Dudley (Governor of Massachusetts 1634, 1640, 1645 and 1650) and also of Gov. Joseph Dudley (Gov. of Massachusetts 1702 to 1715).

She was a woman of rare grace and cheerfulness. In the varied spheres of duty to which she was called she ably fulfilled the requirements of her station." H. C. L.

The Washington correspondent of the New York Times, July 23, 1873, says, "The recent decease of Mrs. Mary Maud Washburn, the wife of Hon. I. Washburn, Jr., of Portland, has brought deep sorrow to a wide circle of family and social friends. Aside from the charming domestic qualities, which rendered her the comfort and idol of her husband and children, she had all the lovely and unaffected attractions that made the society in which she moved in New England and in Washington devoted admirers and more than friends; and her death will be sorrowed over as for the loss of a favorite sister."

Mr. Washburn married, 2d, Robina Napier Brown at Boston, January, 1876. She was the daughter of B. F. Brown of Bangor and was born Sept. 19, 1839. Israel Washburn, Jr., died at Philadelphia, May 12, 1883.

Children of Israel and Mary Maud Washburn, all born at Orono, Maine:

I. ISRAEL HENRY[9], born June 18, 1848. Died at Hot Springs, Arkansas, Feb. 6, 1896.
II. ADA[9], born July 18, 1846.
III. CHARLES FOX[9], born Feb. 19, 1849. Died at Portland, Me., July 11, 1884.
IV. ANNA MAUD[9], born Dec. 23, 1861.

9. ISRAEL HENRY WASHBURN, son of Israel[8], Jr., and Mary Maud Washburn, received an academic education. On the outbreak of the Rebellion, he enlisted in the 16th Maine Regiment,

Company H, Capt. John Ayer. He was on the staff of Gen. Berry when the latter was killed at Chancellorsville. On Nov. 13, 1862, he was commissioned first lieutenant of the company and served till April 16, 1863, when he resigned on account of ill health. He was commissioned second lieutenant on the U. S. Marine Corps, March 18, 1864, and was commissioned captain in same, March 20, 1883. He retired July 15, 1886, for disability incident to the service. After his retirement he made Portsmouth his home. He married at Portsmouth, N. H., June 18, 1867, Arabella V. Jackson, who was born at Portsmouth, May 9, 1846.

Children of same:

I. ISRAEL HENRY[10], born at Portsmouth, N. H., Nov. 10, 1870.
II. MOLLY[10], born at Erie, Penn., May 18, 1873. Died at Portsmouth, March 29, 1875.
III. JACKSON MAURICE[10], born at Portsmouth, Jan. 23, 1879.
IV. CHARLES CADWALLADER[10], born at Charlestown Navy Yard, July 6, 1882.

10. Israel Henry Washburn, Jr., married at Portsmouth, N. H., March 9, 1898, Virginia Sanborn of that city. Their home is at Portsmouth, N. H.

9. Charles Fox Washburn, son of Israel[8] Washburn, Jr., lived in Minnesota and served in both branches of the legislature.

FAMILY OF ALGERNON SIDNEY WASHBURN.

8. ALGERNON SIDNEY WASHBURN, second son of Israel and Martha B. Washburn, was born at Livermore, Nov. 29, 1814.

To his brother Israel's " Notes of Livermore," he, as "Uncle John," makes a contribution which contains the following allusion to his early education:

" The first school-house in the Dr. Bradford district ('The Norlands') was built near the beginning of the century. It was an old-fashioned, square building, with hipped roof and was never painted....And from this primitive old brown, and later old white, school-house, without a word of Latin or Greek, I slid quietly away from the good old neighborhood, while some of the boys more favored, went to the high-schools, academies and colleges.

No wonder that when, at a long subsequent period, a bright and ingenuous youth was hearing others discuss their graduations and degrees, their class days and commencements, and was told that the writer's *Alma Mater* was represented by the old faded school-house, he should have been struck with amazement that one with such scant opportunities should be so wise!"

Algernon Sidney Washburn was in early life a merchant in Boston and later he was a banker in Hallowell, Maine.

He married at Bangor, Me., Jan. 11, 1854, Sarah A. Moore, who was born at Dover, Maine, August 10, 1830. He died at Hallowell, Sept. 29, 1879. His wife died at Hallowell, Feb. 24, 1866.

Family of Algernon Sidney Washburn

Children of same: All born at Hallowell.

I. JAMES[9], born August 25, 1855. Died at Hallowell, June 28, 1866.
II. JOHN[9], born August 1, 1858.
III. ROBERT CHARLES[9], born March 26, 1861.
IV. CADWALLADER[9], born Feb. 10, 1866. Died, March 7, 1866.

9. JOHN WASHBURN, son of Algernon Sidney[8], (Bowdoin, 1882) married at Hallowell, Maine, July 29, 1884, Elizabeth Pope Harding, who was born at Machias, Maine. His home is in Minneapolis, where he is Vice President of the C. C. Washburn Flouring Mills Co.

Children of same, born at Minneapolis, Minn.:

I. MARGARET[10], born May 24, 1885.
II. ELIZABETH POPE[10], born Sept. 16, 1893.

9. ROBERT CHARLES WASHBURN, son of Algernon Sidney[8], (Tufts College, 1883) married at Portland, Oregon, May 8, 1889, Mary Louise Savier, who was born in that city.

He represented the city of Seattle in the Legislature of Washington, 1892, and served in the Senate of Washington, 1894-1896.

FAMILY OF ELIHU BENJAMIN WASHBURNE.

8. ELIHU BENJAMIN WASHBURNE, third son of Israel[1] and Martha Benjamin Washburn, was born at Livermore, Sept. 23, 1816.

He attended the same district school where "Uncle John" graduated and taught a term of school himself, when eighteen years old, for ten dollars a month and "boarded 'round."

When the school closed he went into the office of "The Christian Intelligencer," published at Gardiner, Me., and later into the office of "The Kennebec Journal" at Augusta, Me. Here he formed a lasting friendship with Luther Severance, the editor. Mr. Severance had been in the office of the "National Intelligencer" of Washington before coming to Augusta, where he established the first paper of the city, "The Kennebec Journal," in 1824. He was at one time a member of Congress, and was sent by President Fillmore in 1850 as United States Commissioner to the Sandwich Islands for four years. He died of cancer immediately after his return to Augusta, in 1855. His warm friendship for Mr. Severance led Mr. Washburne to place his portrait in the Washburn Memorial Library at "The Norlands," in 1887.

In 1836 E. B. Washburne entered Kent's Hill Seminary at Readfield, Me., where he had as school-fellows, Timothy O. Howe, late U. S. Senator from Wisconsin, Rev. William R. French, D. D., Rev. James P. Weston, D. D., late President of Lombard University, all life-long friends.

Family of Elihu Benjamin Washburne 55

In 1839 he entered the Cambridge Law School and had as Professors, Justice Story and Simon Greenleaf, and as classmates Gen. Charles Devens, Ex-Gov. Bullock, Richard H. Dana, Jr., James Russell Lowell, W. W. Story and William M. Evarts.

In 1840 he went to Illinois and began the practice of law with Charles S. Hempstead of Galena.

In 1852 he was elected to Congress and was kept there continuously sixteen years, being at the time of his retirement " Father of the House," in which capacity he swore into office Schuyler Colfax and James G. Blaine as Speakers of the House.

To Mr. Washburne and Mr. Seward alone was confided the secret of the train by which Mr. Lincoln would reach Washington for his first inaugural, the telegraph wire being cut when he left Philadelphia that the event might not be communicated to the enemy then in arms. Mr. Seward failed in keeping the appointment, and Mr. Washburne met Mr. Lincoln alone at the Baltimore & Ohio depot.

Gen. Grant, who was one of Mr. Washburne's constituents, was much indebted for his early position and advancement in the Civil War to Mr. Washburne's friendship and influence. This favor he acknowledged and returned when as President in 1869 he offered Mr. Washburne a seat in his Cabinet as Secretary of State.

This office Mr. Washburne soon resigned and accepted that of Minister to France, which he held during the two terms of Gen. Grant's administration. This period covered the Franco-German war and Mr. Washburne remained in Paris during the siege by the Prussians and the reign of the Commune.

The term of service was eight and a half years, the longest of any diplomatic representation from America to France.

After his return to America Mr. Washburne wrote "The Recollections of a Minister to France," a vivid picture of all he had experienced in those eventful years.

John – Margaret Moore
s Jos – Hannah Latham
s Jos – Hannah Johnson
s. Ebenezer – Dorothy Newhall
s Cyrus – Electra Stratton
        Rhoda Field – Lucy Hathaway
s Edwin – Eliz. Bascom
s Percy – Nettie Search
s Claude – Ann Jameson
s. David – Joan Callahan

David Washburn
4-22-62

WASHBURN MEMORIAL LIBRARY.

In 1885 a beautiful granite Library was erected at "The Norlands" by E. B. Washburne and his brother, W. D. Washburn of Minneapolis, for the free use of Livermore and East Livermore.

In this Library were placed about five thousand volumes, the gift of the family of Israel Washburn, Jr., of Portland. There are also hung in this Library fine portraits in oil of Israel[7] Washburn, Martha Benjamin Washburn, Israel[8] Washburn, Jr., Algernon Sidney[8] Washburn, Elihu B.[5] Washburne, C. C.[8] Washburn, William D.[8] Washburn, Reuel[7] Washburn, Mr. and Mrs. David Benjamin, Mr. and Mrs. Samuel Morison, Dr. Benjamin Bradford, William Henry Brettun, Otis Pray, Dr. Cyrus Hamlin, Hannibal Hamlin, Luther Severance and John Brown.

A number of these portraits are by the celebrated artist, G. P. A. Healy.

At the dedication of this Library (Aug. 5, 1885) Mr. Washburne said:

"To mark our veneration for our parents, and as a slight testimonial of all we owe them, there has been erected on my own behalf and on behalf of my brothers and sisters, a building to be known as 'The Washburn Memorial Library,' and is here to-day solemnly dedicated to the memory of Israel and Martha Benjamin Washburn."

8. Elihu B. Washburne married at Gratiot's Grove (near Shullsburg) Wisconsin, July 31, 1845, Adèle Gratiot, daughter of

Henry Gratiot. She was born at Fevre River (now Galena), Illinois, Nov. 12, 1826.

Mrs. Washburne's grandfather, Charles Gratiot, was born at Lausanne, Switzerland, whither his parents had fled on the revocation of the edict of Nantes when all Huguenots were driven out of France. Charles Gratiot came to America and served the cause of the American Revolution with great devotion.

After her death, a window in memory of Mrs. Adèle Gratiot Washburne was placed in the Huguenot church of Charleston, S. C., and one in the Universalist Church at "The Norlands," Livermore.

The mother of Mrs. Washburne was Susan Hempstead of St. Louis, daughter of Stephen Hempstead of Connecticut, who was a soldier of the Revolutionary War, as were the other three great-grandfathers of Mrs. Washburn's children.

"Mrs. Washburne was one," said Prof. Swing, "whose life reached out in a strange manner and touched the world in many places and in different times....an ideal woman of our country."

After Mr. Washburne's return from France his home was in Chicago where he died Oct. 22, 1887, aged 71 years. His wife died at Chicago March 18, 1887, aged 60 years.

Children of Elihu B.[8] and Adèle Gratiot Washburne:

I. Infant son born at Galena, Ill., Apr. 15, 1846. Died Apr. 22, 1846.
II. GRATIOT[9], born at Galena, May 6, 1849. Died at Louisville, Kentucky, Dec. 17, 1886.
III. HEMPSTEAD[9], born at Galena Nov. 11, 1851.
IV. WILLIAM PITT[9], born at Washington, D. C., April 22, 1854. Died at Galveston, Texas, November 23, 1898.

Children of Elihu B.[8] Washburne

V. ELIHU BENJAMIN[9], Jr., born at Raynham, Mass., July 28, 1857. "Bennie" died at Galena, Jan. 27, 1862.
VI. SUSAN ADELE[9], born at Raynham, Mass., April 21, 1859.
VII. MARIE LISA[9], born at Galena, Ill., Aug. 17, 1863.
VIII. ELIHU BENJAMIN[9], Jr., born at Washington, D. C., Nov. 16, 1868.

9. GRATIOT WASHBURNE, son of Elihu B. Washburne, was for a time at the Highland Military Academy at Worcester, Mass., and at the Naval Academy at Newport, R. I. Later he entered and graduated from the State Normal University of Illinois.

He was second Secretary of the United States Legation while his father was Minister to France. At the close of the Franco-Prussian war he was one of four Americans, of the American Ambulance, who were decorated with the Cross of the Legion of Honor by the French government for valuable services performed during the siege and Commune of Paris. Upon his return to the United States he entered the Custom House of New York, and at the time of his death was Secretary of the Management of the American Exposition which opened the following year in London, England.

He died suddenly at Louisville, Kentucky, Dec. 17, 1886, aged 37 years.

9. HEMPSTEAD WASHBURNE, son of Elihu B.,[8] fitted for college at Kent's Hill, Maine, passed the Bowdoin examinations and went to Europe in 1871. He took a two years' course at the University of Bonn, and returning to the United States was graduated from the Law School of the University of Wisconsin,

1874, and from the Union College of Law, Chicago, in 1875. He has had as law partners Hon. Lyman Trumbull, H. S. Robbins and Theodore Brentano

He was Master in Chancery of the Superior Court of Cook County five years, City Attorney of Chicago four years and Mayor of Chicago 1891-1893. He is now a member of the Civil Service Commission of Chicago.

Hempstead Washburne married at Chicago June 28, 1883, Annie M. Clarke, who was born in that city.

Children of same: all born in Chicago.

I. ADELE BERTRAND[10], born Apr. 14, 1884. Died May 14, 1884.
II. CLARK[10], born March 18, 1885.
III. GRATIOT[10], born July 4, 1889.
IV. HEMPSTEAD, JR.,[10] born Dec. 25, 1891.
V. ANNETTE[10], born at Chicago, Oct. 6, 1898.

9. William Pitt Washburne, son of E. B. Washburne[8], was born at Washington, D. C., Apr. 22, 1854. He accompanied his father to Paris in 1869. After several years in preparatory schools in France and Germany, he passed the Sorbonne examinations at Paris and entered the National Academy of Medicine of France where he remained two years. He was also at the branch Medical School at Montpelier in the south of France. He returned to this country at the expiration of his father's mission to France.

He married 1st at Livermore Jan. 1, 1887, Cora Rose Hinds, and 2d at Galveston July 5, 1898, Mrs. Lula Grace Buise of Syracuse, New York.

His home was in Galveston, Texas.

9. Susan Adèle Washburne, daughter of Elihu B.[8] and Adèle Gratiot Washburne, received her education in the schools of Chicago, Paris and Bonn.

She married at Chicago, Ill., Feb. 1, 1882, William D. Bishop, Jr., who was born at Bridgeport, Conn., Dec. 16, 1857, and graduated at Yale 1880.

Children of same: Born in Bridgeport.

I. NATALIE WASHBURNE[10], born Sept. 18, 1885.

II. WILLIAM D. BISHOP 3d, born June 21, 1889.

9. Marie Lisa Washburne, daughter of Elihu B.[8] and Adèle Gratiot Washburne was educated at the same schools as her sister and was also in Boston select schools three years.

She married at "The Norlands," Livermore, Me., Oct. 7, 1885, A. H. Fowler of Denver, Col., who was born at Guilford, Conn., Aug. 13, 1851. Mr. Fowler was educated at Guilford and New Haven and went to Colorado in 1878.

Children of same: Born at Denver, Col.

I. ELIHU WASHBURNE[10], born Oct. 28, 1886.

II. JOHN ELIOT[10], born Sept. 29, 1890.

III. SALLY ADELE WASHBURNE[10], born Feb. 4, 1898.

FAMILY OF CADWALLADER COLDEN WASHBURN.

8. CADWALLADER COLDEN WASHBURN, son of Israel[7] and Martha Benjamin Washburn, was born at Livermore, Apr. 22, 1818.

He studied law and settled at Mineral Point, Wisconsin, in 1842.

In 1854 he was elected to Congress as a Whig, and was re-elected as a Republican the two succeeding terms, when he declined a re-election.

On the breaking out of the war of the Rebellion, he entered the service as Col. of the 2d Wisconsin Cavalry in 1861. He was made Brig. Gen'l June, 1862, and Major General Nov., 1862.

In 1866 he was again elected to Congress and again in 1868.

In 1871 he was elected Governor of Wisconsin for two years.

He founded the Washburn flouring mills of Minneapolis.

Mr. Washburn amassed a large fortune which he gave very generously in private and public bequests. His largest public gifts were: The Washburn Observatory, Madison, Wis., $50,000. Edgewood School for girls, his private residence at Madison given to the Sisters of Charity, $20,000. The Washburn "Home" for Orphans, Minneapolis, Minnesota, $375,000.

The last named gift he referred to as follows: "I wish to leave some memorial behind me of my devoted mother. I have thought I could do no better than to establish in her memory a home for orphan children."

This Asylum was opened for the reception of children Nov.

Family of Cadwallader C. Washburn

16, 1886, and the report of 1892 states that an average of eighty-five children had been cared for at the Home during that year.

8. Cadwallader C. Washburn married at Mineral Point, Wisconsin, Jan. 1, 1849, Jeannette Garr who was born at New York City June 9, 1818.

He died at Eureka Springs, Arkansas, May 14, 1882, aged 64
Children of same:

I. JEANNETTE GARR[9]. Born at Mineral Point, Wis., Apr. 25, 1850.

II. FANNY[9]. Born at New York City March 23, 1852.

9. Jeannette Garr Washburn, daughter of Cadwallader C. Washburn, married at La Crosse, Wisconsin, June 23, 1869, Albert Warren Kelsey who was born at Boston, Mass., Oct. 30, 1840. Their home is in Philadelphia.

Children of same:

I. ALBERT[10], born at St. Louis, Missouri, Apr. 26, 1870.

II. JEANNETTE[10], born at St. Louis, Mo., Nov. 1, 1871. Died at Madison, Wis., Aug. 3, 1872.

III. CHARLOTTE[10], born at Madison, Wis., Oct. 28, 1873.

IV. KATE[10], born at Madison, Wis., Apr. 23, 1875.

V. MARY[10], born at St. Louis, Mo., June 15, 1877.

VI. MABEL[10], born at Geneva, Switzerland, Oct. 16, 1878.

VII. KARL[10], born at Clarence, Switzerland, July 30, 1880.

VIII. ETHEL[10], born at Meredith, New Hampshire, Aug. 17, 1882.

IX. BONNIBEL[10], born at Philadelphia, Pa., Feb. 15, 1884.

Mr. A. W. Kelsey was educated at Chapman Hall, Boston, and during the residence of his father's family in Maine he

attended the Lewiston Falls Academy. Mrs. Kelsey attended private schools in Boston and vicinity and was a short time at Westbrook Seminary.

Their son, Albert Kelsey, was educated in Europe and at Ury House and St. Luke's schools near Philadelphia. He studied architecture, and was elected President of the T Square Club in 1896. In the same year he gained the travelling scholarship of architecture of the University of Pennsylvania. During the following year and a half he travelled in Europe and the Orient, meantime going on with his architectural notes, drawings, sketches and studies, called the Science of Cities.

He represented the T Square Club at the IV. International Congress of Architects held in Brussels in 1897, when he addressed the members in French, his speech being subsequently published in the *Compte rendu* of the Congress. He is a member of the firm of Kennedy, Hays and Kelsey of Philadelphia.

10. Albert Kelsey married at New York City, Jan. 18, 1899, Henrietta Latitia Allis of that city.

Mrs. Kelsey's daughters have been educated at home under private instruction mostly. Karl Kelsey is in the Manual Training School of Philadelphia.

9. Fanny Washburn, daughter of C. C. and Jeannette Garr Washburn, married at Madison, Wisconsin, June 5, 1872, Charles Payson, who was born at Messina, Sicily, of American parents, May 2, 1837. Mr. Payson graduated at Trinity College, Cambridge, England. Their home is in Washington, D. C.

Children of same: All born at Washington, D. C.
I. EDITH WASHBURN, born July 24, 1873.
II. JEANNETTE GARR, born Jan. 9, 1875.
III. FRANCES LITHGOW, born Jan. 8, 1878.

10. Jeannette Garr Payson, daughter of Charles and Fanny Washburn Payson, married at Washington, D. C., Oct. 28, 1895, Raymond Le Ghait, Secretary of the Belgian Legation and son of the Belgian Minister at Washington.

Child of same:
I. MARGUERITE, born in Paris, France, Nov. 21, 1896.

10. Frances Lithgow Payson, daughter of Charles and Fanny Washburn[9] Payson, married at Paris, France, July 29, 1896, Pierre Botkine of the Russian Diplomatic Service.

FAMILY OF MARTHA WASHBURN STEPHENSON.

8. MARTHA BENJAMIN WASHBURN, oldest daughter of Israel[7] and Martha Benjamin Washburn, was born at Livermore, Maine, Feb. 6, 1820. She was educated in the schools of Livermore and at Waterville Liberal Institute.

She married at Mineral Point, Wisconsin, June 6, 1849, Capt. Charles L. Stephenson, who was born at Gorham, Maine, Apr. 13, 1815, and who died at St. Paul, Minnesota, Aug. 31, 1880.

Children of same:

I. ELIZABETH CHAMPLAIN[9]. Born at Mineral Point, Wis., May 24, 1850.

II. FREDERIC WILLIAM[9]. Born at Mineral Point, Wis., Feb. 21, 1853.

III. MARTHA EUGENIE[9]. Born at Galena, Illinois, Dec. 13, 1854.

IV. BENJAMIN WASHBURN[9]. Born at Galena, Ill., June 10, 1857. Died at Galena, Ill., Sept. 5, 1859.

V. BENJAMIN WASHBURN[9]. Born at Galena, Ill., Oct. 1, 1860.

9. ELIZABETH C. STEPHENSON was educated at the schools of Galena and at the Seminaries at Gorham and Westbrook, Maine, and at Monticello, Illinois.

9. FREDERIC WILLIAM STEPHENSON was educated at the schools of Galena and at Gorham Seminary.

He married at La Crosse, Wisconsin, April 27, 1885, Mrs. Eliza E. Hand. Their home is in Chicago.

9. MARTHA EUGENIA STEPHENSON was educated at Galena and at Gorham and Monticello Seminaries. She married at St Paul, Minnesota, Oct. 19, 1887, D. Jonas Lucas.

FAMILY OF CHARLES AMES WASHBURN.

8. CHARLES AMES WASHBURN, son of Israel[7] and Martha Benjamin Washburn, was born at Livermore, March 16, 1822 He was graduated at Bowdoin College in 1848.

He went to California in 1849 and soon became the editor and publisher of the " Alta Californian " and later of " The Times." In 1860 he was elector at large from California and brought the vote of that State for Lincoln to Washington, D. C.

In 1861 he was appointed by President Lincoln Minister Resident to Paraguay. He was there during the war between that country and Brazil, Uruguay and the Argentine Republic. The lives of Mr. Washburn and his family being in peril, the United States sent the transport " Wasp " to take them away.

After his return to the United States he wrote a very full history of Paraguay. He also wrote two novels, "Philip Thaxter" and "Gomery of Montgomery," and a treatise on "Political Evolution," besides contributing to the current literature of the day.

He died at New York City, Jan. 26, 1889, aged 66 years, 10 mos. 10 days.

8. CHARLES A. WASHBURN married at New York, May 11, 1865, Sallie Catherine Cleaveland, who was born at Reading, Penn., Sept. 17, 1842.

Children of same:

I. HESTER[9], born at Asuncion, Paraguay, Oct. 22, 1867.

II. Thurlow⁹, born at "The Norlands," Livermore, Me., March 16, 1869.

III. Lilian⁹, born at Reading, Pennsylvania, Sept. 27, 1870.

9. Hester Washburn, daughter of Charles A. Washburn, married at Boston, Mass., Oct. 24, 1893, Willis Kirkpatrick Howell, who was born at Morristown, New Jersey, Oct. 13, 1860. Their home is at Morristown, N. J.

Children of same:

I. Willis Washburn¹⁰, born at Morristown, N. J., March 7, 1895.

II. Lawrence Benjamin¹⁰, born at Morristown, N. J., Dec. 27, 1897.

9. Thurlow Washburn was graduated at the Massachusetts Institute of Technology in 1897. He is in New Mexico.

FAMILY OF SAMUEL BENJAMIN WASHBURN.

8. SAMUEL BENJAMIN WASHBURN, son of Israel[7] and Martha Benjamin Washburn, was born at Livermore, Me., Jan. 1, 1824.

In 1842 he went to sea before the mast and two years later he was master of a vessel. He was engaged in the merchant marine service between Boston and Liverpool and between Boston and New Orleans.

He was a captain in the volunteer service of the navy in the late Civil war; and while on the Galena participating in the fight at Fort Darling, May 13, 1862, he was struck on the hip by a round shot and badly wounded, from the effects of which he suffered till his death.

He was afterward in the Gulf Squadron under Admiral Farragut and had command of a division; and in the latter part of 1865 he was in the Atlantic Squadron near the Chesapeake.

After the war he lived a few years in the West and later spent several years at the family homestead, "The Norlands," in Livermore.

In 1887 he went to the Sanitarium at Avon Springs, New York, for medical treatment and died there March 4, 1890, aged 66 years.

8. SAMUEL BENJAMIN WASHBURN married at Le Roy, New York, March 31, 1862, Lorette May Thompson, who died at Owatouna, Minnesota, Feb. 14, 1869. He married, 2d, at East

Livermore, Maine, Jan. 11, 1872, Addie Brown Reade, who was born at Lewiston, Maine, Sept. 21, 1846.

Children of Samuel Benjamin[8] and Lorette M. Washburn:

I. SAMUEL BENJAMIN[9], Jr., born at Le Roy, N. Y., Dec. 27, 1862.
II. SIDNEY[9], who died in infancy.
III. GREENLEAF WHITTIER[9], who died in infancy.

Children of Samuel Benjamin and Addie Reade Washburn.

IV. MARY LORETTE[9], born at "The Norlands," Livermore, Dec. 18, 1873. Died at Livermore, July 5, 1875.
V. KATHERINE BENJAMIN[9], born at "The Norlands," Livermore. Nov. 8, 1876.

9. SAMUEL BENJAMIN WASHBURN, Jr., was educated in the schools of Livermore, Farmington, and Westbrook Seminary. He married at Minneapolis, March 12, 1895, Fanny Henderson of that city. His home is in Minneapolis and he is connected with the Washburn flouring mills there.

9. KATHERINE BENJAMIN WASHBURN, daughter of Samuel Benjamin[8] Washburn, was educated at Granger Place School, Canandaigua, and passed the Vassar examination there in 1895.

She married at Avon, New York, June 15, 1898, John Francis Kellogg, who was born at Avon, June 4, 1871.

Their home is at Avon, New York.

FAMILY OF MARY WASHBURN BUFFUM.

8. Mary Benjamin Washburn, second daughter of Israel[7] and Martha B. Washburn, was born at Livermore, Nov. 11, 1825.

She married at Livermore, March 29, 1858, Gustavus A. Buffum, who was born at Palermo, Maine, Dec. 26, 1825.

She died at Lyons, Iowa, March 15, 1867.

Children of same:

I. Frank Washburn[9], born at Monroe, Wis., July 1, 1859.

II. Ada Mary[9], born at Lyons, Iowa, Feb. 5, 1862.

III. Charles Gustavus[9], born at Lyons, Iowa, April 19, 1865.

IV. Cadwallader Washburn[9], born at Lyons, Iowa, March 5, 1867.

V. Benjamin Washburn[9], born at Lyons, Iowa, March 5, 1867. Both twins died at Lyons, Iowa, September, 1867.

9. Frank Washburn Buffum, son of G. A. and Mary Washburn[8] Buffum, attended Ingleside College, Palmyra, Missouri. He married at Louisiana, Mo., March 18, 1893, Margaret V. Smith, who was born at Pike Co., Missouri, June 4, 1869, and who died at Louisiana, Mo., March 15, 1895.

9. Ada Mary Buffum, daughter of Gustavus A. and Mary Washburn[8] Buffum, educated at Monticello Seminary, Godfrey, Illinois. Married at Louisiana, Mo., Dec. 9, 1885, David Arthur Stuart, who was born at Danville, Mo., Sept. 26, 1848, and died at Denver, Colorado, Jan. 27, 1889.

She married, 2d, at Louisiana, Mo., James Ovid Stark of Stark, Missouri, April 28, 1897.

Child of same:

I. MARY ROXANA[10], born at Stark, Mo., Dec. 1, 1898.

9. CHARLES GUSTAVUS BUFFUM, son of G. A. and Mary Washburn Buffum, attended Jacksonville Business College and other schools. He married at Kansas City, Missouri, June 1, 1893, Gertrude Emily Carkiner, who was born at Danville, Mo., Jan. 11, 1868.

Child of same:

I. MARY FRANCES[10], born at Louisiana, Missouri, May 30, 1898.

FAMILY OF WILLIAM DREW WASHBURN.

8. WILLIAM DREW WASHBURN, the eighth and only surviving son of Israel[7] and Martha Benjamin Washburn, was born at Livermore, Jan. 14, 1831.

He was graduated at Bowdoin College in 1854, studied law and settled in Minneapolis, Minnesota, May, 1857. He represented the city of Minneapolis in the State Legislature in 1858-7 *71*, and from 1861 to 1865 he was U. S. Surveyor-General for Minnesota.

He was a member of Congress from 1879 to 1885 and in 1889 was elected to the United States Senate.

He has been extensively interested in timber lands, mill property and railroads in the northwest.

He gave the site on which stands the orphans' "Home," at Minneapolis, which was given by his brother, Cadwallader C. Washburn; and he has been President of the board of trustees of that institution since its opening in 1886.

He married at Bangor, Maine, April 19, 1859, Elizabeth Little Muzzy, who was born at Bangor, June 27, 1836.

Children of same:

I. FRANKLIN MUZZY[9], born at Minneapolis, Minn., May 4, 1861. Drowned at Scarboro' Beach, Maine, July 29, 1877.

II. WILLIAM DREW, Jr.[9], born at St. Paul, Minn., Apr. 3, 1863.

III. CADWALLADER LINCOLN[9], born at Minneapolis, Oct. 31, 1866.

IV. MARY CAROLINE[9], born at Minneapolis, Minn., Aug. 31, 1868.

V. EDWIN CHAPIN[9], born at Minneapolis, Apr. 11, 1870.

VI. GEORGE HENRY[9], born at Minneapolis, Dec. 24, 1871. Died at Minneapolis, Feb. 11, 1872.

VII. ELIZABETH[9], born at Minneapolis Nov. 19, 1874.

VIII. STANLEY[9], born at Minneapolis Feb. 7, 1878.

IX. ALICE[9], born at Minneapolis July 11, 1881. Died at Minneapolis Aug. 29, 1881.

9. WILLIAM DREW WASHBURN, Jr., (Yale, '88) married at Portland, Oregon, Sept. 25, 1890, Florence Agnes Savier, who was born at Portland, Oregon, August 16, 1868.

Children of same:

I. BEATRICE[10], born at Chicago, Ill., June 26, 1891.

II. WILLIAM DREW, 3d[10], born at Minneapolis July 28, 1897.

9. CADWALLADER LINCOLN WASHBURN, son of William Drew[8] Washburn, was graduated at Gallaudet College, Washington, D. C., 1890, and was a member of the class of 1893 at the Massachusetts Institute of Technology. He is an artist by profession. He sent to the Paris Salon in 1897 a picture called " Une Marche du Tanger." At the close of the exhibition Mr. Washburn was requested by the Chicago Art Institute to loan it to their winter exhibition. In 1898 he had a picture in the Champs de Mars exhibition called " Une Fille "—a small child getting ready for a bath.

9. MARY CAROLINE WASHBURN, daughter of W. D. Washburn, graduated at Ogoutz School, 1888. She married at Min-

neapolis Nov. 23, 1892, Elbert Francis Baldwin of New York, a graduate of Williams College.

Children of same:

I. ELBERT[10], born in New York Feb. 12, 1894.

II. MARIAN, born in New York June 5, 1895.

9. EDWIN CHAPIN WASHBURN entered Yale College, 1891. Was injured in foot-ball and left at end of first year.

9. STANLEY WASHBURN entered Williams College 1897.

FAMILY OF CAROLINE WASHBURN HOLMES.

8. CAROLINE ANN WASHBURN, youngest daughter of Israel[7] and Martha Benjamin Washburn, was born at Livermore January 30, 1833. She was educated at the schools of Livermore, Waterville Liberal Institute and Gorham Seminary.

She married at Livermore June 3, 1857, Dr. Freeland S. Holmes, who was born at Foxcroft, Me., Sept. 8, 1827. Dr. Holmes graduated at Bowdoin College, 1850, and from the Medical School at Washington, D. C.

He joined the army in March, 1862, as Surgeon of the Sixth Regiment of Maine Volunteers and died in the service, at Germantown, Virginia, June 23, 1863.

Children of same: Born at Foxcroft, Maine.

I. FANNY WASHBURN[9], born July 3, 1859.
II. FRANK EDWARD[9], born June 8, 1862.

9. FANNY W. HOLMES was educated at the schools of Minneapolis and at Miss Morgan's School, Portsmouth, N. H.

9. FRANK E. HOLMES graduated from Phillips Academy, Andover, Mass.

Their home is in Minneapolis, Minn.

FAMILY OF MOLLY WASHBURN LEONARD.

7. MOLLY WASHBURN, oldest daughter of Israel[6] and Abiah King Washburn, was born at Raynham, Mass., Nov. 14, 1786. One very near to her writes this of her: "She was a model of home duty—ever responsive to the call of neighbor, town or country; loving literature, but *Duty* most of all."

She married at Raynham, Aug. 13, 1815, Payton Randolph Leonard.

After her marriage she lived in the old "Gothic house" built in 1670, in which five generations of Leonards had been born, her own children being the sixth and last. It was in this fine mansion, then almost new, that the escort was entertained over night that conveyed the head of King Philip to Plymouth from Mount Hope, where Philip was slain Aug. 12, 1676. [As the head was deposited in the cellar over night, this family may be said literally to have had a King's head under their feet.]

James Leonard, the first of the name in this country, came to Taunton, Mass., from Pontypool, Wales, where he had been connected with an iron bloomary; and near his house in Taunton (now Raynham) he set up the first iron forge in America in 1652. The Leonard residence in Raynham still bears the name of "Pontypool."

The Leonard family originated in Kent, England, and occupied Hurstmanceaux Castle four hundred years, the head of the family and title being Lord Dacre, mentioned by Scott in Rokeby.

Family of Molly Washburn Leonard

The ruins of Hurstmanceaux Castle, ivy covered, are among the most picturesque in England.

Miss Amy Leonard of Raynham tells the following anecdote of her two great-grandfathers, Zephaniah Leonard and Israel[3] Washburn, both men of prominence in their day.

Her great-grandfather Leonard had been for many years chosen Moderator at the annual town-meetings of Raynham; but one day, he being late, her great-grandfather Washburn was chosen. Mr. Leonard soon appeared and walked up to the desk as if to take his accustomed place, with an air of right and superiority.

Mr. Washburn held his ground, however, and said in a dry manner, "No doubt but you are the people and wisdom will die with you; but I have understanding as well as you. I am not inferior to you,"* and *he continued to preside*.

Payton Randolph Leonard was born in Raynham, Dec. 12, 1775, and died there Dec. 22, 1843. Molly Washburn[7] Leonard died at Raynham Aug. 7, 1874, aged 87 years, 8 mos. 23 days.

Children of same:

I. AMY[8], born in Raynham Oct. 9, 1818.

II. OLIVE[8], born in Raynham Sept. 3, 1820. Died at Raynham (Easter morning) Apr. 17, 1881.

III. LYDIA WASHBURN[8], born at Raynham May 22, 1823. Died at Raynham Nov. 17, 1848.

8. AMY LEONARD, the oldest daughter of Payson Randolph and Molly Washburn Leonard, attended Bristol Academy and graduated from the State Normal School at Bridgewater, Mass.

*Job xii: 2, 3.

She has much interest in the cause of Temperance and has been President and Chaplain of a branch of the W. C. T. U. for sixteen years. She was a nurse in the Civil war and was associated in her work with Miss Dix.

From Point of Rocks, Va., Jan. 18, 1865, she writes:

"This hospital is on an elevated spot about sixty feet above the turbid waters of the Appomattox. It is designed to be a hospital for ten thousand patients. At present three thousand are cared for here in the barracks already finished, and in the cloth tents.

* * * * * *

"Now I will take you to my ward which is in a tent, whose cloth sides seem but a poor shelter for the sick. Here beside a big burly man with wild eyes and a forest of whiskers lies a pretty pink-faced boy, with mild blue eyes and a thoughtful, refined expression. 'I am glad you have come,' said he, 'I was looking for you so long.' 'And how are you to-day?' 'Oh, so sick.'

* * * * * *

"Jan.—A bright lovely day. Two new patients came in to-day. One, on seeing me, seemed to be carried in spirit to his home, for he said with tearful eyes, 'Oh, my poor wife! how will she feel when she knows that I am here.' I combed the Maine boy's hair, gave him a pocket handkerchief, wrote for him a letter and tried to comfort him.

"Another little whitehead told me he was seventeen. 'Why didn't you stay at home with your mother?' 'Oh, the other boys were coming and so I wanted to.'

"Jan.—A trying day. I was told this morning Frank was ordered to Fortress Monroe. I was glad for him; but I had

watched over the good, patient, handsome boy for three months, fed him like an infant for weeks, had been called 'Mother' by him, in his delirium, 'Saint, angel, darling,' etc., and could not see him go without a tear. I left him packed into the ambulance and would have gone to the boat, but I knew there was a dying boy who was looking for me and who had said to me that morning, 'I am glad when you come and sorry when you go.' So I hastened to the fair boy who has the awkward name of Gideon and who too calls me 'Mother, dear mother.'"

"Feb. 17, 1865. All goes quietly along—sick boys in bleak tents. Some recover, some die and some linger on. They are generally patient, respectful, some thankful, although a good many forget the little signs of gratitude; but I feel not unrewarded though no 'thank you' should be mine. I feel if I can give my mite to God and my country it is compensation enough. I feel that while grim war scowls on our fair land I will do my best to alleviate its horrors."

She made good her words and stayed to the end of the war, but came home stricken with army fever and for many weeks it was thought she would not live.

A few years after the war Miss Leonard adopted a daughter —Lois Dean Gushee—whom she educated. This daughter married Albert James Park of Taunton and they have three children, Leonard, Gladys and Esther. Their home is at Worcester.

8. OLIVE, daughter of Payton Randolph and Molly Washburn[7] Leonard, was educated at Bristol Academy, Taunton, and the schools of Raynham. She married at Raynham, Oct. 24,

1847, Theodore Foster of New York. Mr. Foster was born at Machias, Me., Oct. 21, 1811. He was a journalist and was at one time on the editorial staff of the New York Tribune. He went to California in January, 1849. The following lines were written by Mrs. Foster in October, 1849.

> "Pale was the winter sun, and keen
>   The winter wind that day,
> That filled the Marah's snowy sails
>   And bore my love away.
> But colder than the northern blast,
>   That round the vessel blew,
> Sank down into my aching heart
>   The parting word, adieu.
>   *   *   *   *   *   *
> Anon the winter snows were gone;
>   Spring brought the violets back;
> But not the wanderer bound afar
>   O'er ocean's stormy track.
> And summer passed, all rich in bloom,
>   And song of bird and bee,—
> But who can tell me if my love
>   Will e'er come back to me?"

[Alas! he came not back, but died in California Aug. 28, 1853.]

The following hymn is taken from a manuscript volume of occasional poems by Mrs. Foster:

Christmas Hymn—1864.

> We know why the bells to-night are ringing,
> And the choral bands to-night are singing,
> We know why the lamps to-night are shining,
> And the cedar and holly the cross are twining.

And the children know, and the mothers know,
    And the soldier lad afar,
Keeping his lonely watch to-night,
    Is thinking of Bethlehem's Star.

We know why the drum to-night is beating,
And hosts in the battle's shock are meeting,
And the brave men know, who their lives are giving
For freedom and country, that Christ is living.
    And the prisoner knows, in his martyr den,
    And the weary, waiting slave—
    And the sailor afloat on the tossing main,
    Who it is that cometh to save.

While the light of the stars to-night is falling,
We know that the Shepherd of Souls is calling—
And he bids, in tones of divinest pleading
To the fields of peace where his lambs are feeding;
    Mothers and children and soldiers brave,
    And they that in prisons pine,
    The sailor at sea and the patient slave,
    Dear Saviour, they all are thine.
        —OLIVE LEONARD FOSTER.

FAMILY OF BENJAMIN WASHBURN.

7. BENJAMIN WASHBURN, son of Israel[6] and Abiah King Washburn, was born at Raynham, Mass., Feb. 10, 1791. He went to Ohio when a young man. It is said that he wished to take a Raynham wife there, but the parents of the young lady chosen would not consent to her going so *far out of the world as Ohio* to make a home.

He married at Greenfield, Ohio, and lived there till his death, which occurred July 1, 1830. His wife died in 1853.

Children of same:

I. LYDIA HELEN[8].
II. MINERVA.[8]

8. LYDIA HELEN WASHBURN married Dr. Clark and went to California. She died at San Luis Obispo. She had children, but their names are not known.

Minerva married and her husband died about 1853.

It is thought that no descendants of Benjamin[7] Washburn are living. (1898.)

FAMILY OF REUEL WASHBURN.

7. REUEL WASHBURN, son of Israel[6] and Abiah King Washburn, was born at Raynham, Mass., May 21, 1793. He was graduated at Brown University in 1814. He read law with Gov. Albion Keith Parris, at Paris, Me., and was admitted to the bar of Oxford County in 1818.

He soon came to Livermore where his brother Israel[7] was living, and settled at North Livermore, which continued to be his home till his death, except one year (1851-52) which he spent in Oshkosh, Wis.

He was Register of Probate for Oxford County from 1821 to 1823. He was State Senator in 1827 and 1828 and a member of Gov. Enoch Lincoln's Council in 1829.

He was nominated for Congress by the Whig party in 1828, and lost the election by but five votes (and those said to have been irregularly cast).

He was Representative to the Legislature five years between 1832 and 1841, and Judge of Probate for Androscoggin County from 1857 to 1859, when he resigned. He died at town-meeting March 4, 1878. He had just spoken vigorously upon some matter which was before the meeting, and sitting down, immediately expired.

At a meeting of the Androscoggin Bar after his death, Judge Walton said: " It is neither just to the dead nor useful to the

living to give exaggerated or indiscriminate eulogy......but in speaking of the moral worth of Judge Washburn, there is no language too strong."

Senator William P. Frye said: "When Reuel Washburn was Judge of Probate I had the honor to serve him as the Register; I learned to know him well, and the good God never made a nobler nor an honester man."

Rev. Dr. Snow wrote: "Mr. Washburn always seemed to me to represent more fully and more purely than any other man I ever knew that ideal type of character and manners which we associate with the old-time 'Gentleman.'"

Hon. Josiah Drummond of Portland wrote: "The news of his death is received here with sorrow; he is mourned as a great and good man and Mason."

Gov. Israel Washburn, Jr., in a sketch of his life said: "He was a well-grounded and sincere Christian. He was a pillar of strength in the organization to which in early life he attached himself. He had no doubt of the final triumph of good over evil or of the ultimate cleansing and elevation of all souls......He died as he had wished to die with the harness on, and among the people he had served so faithfully, and whom he loved as a father loves his children.

'Felix, non vitæ tantum claritate,
sed etiam opportunitate mortis!'*

7. REUEL WASHBURN married at Raynham, Mass., Oct. 19,

---

*Happy, not only from the purity of his life, but also from the opportuneness of his death.

1820, Delia King*, daughter of Barzillai and Nelly McCloud King. She was born at Raynham, May 14, 1801, and died at Livermore, Sept. 25, 1886, aged 85 yrs. 4 mos. 11 days. He died March 4, 1878, aged 84 yrs. 9 mos. 11 days.

Children of same:

I. HARRIET[8], born at Livermore, Jan. 25, 1822. Died at Livermore, Dec. 29, 1888.

II. GANEM W.[8], born at Livermore, Oct. 29, 1823.

III. ALONZO[8], born at Livermore, June 3, 1826.

IV. SETH[8], born at Livermore, March 30, 1829. Died at Livermore August 13, 1830.

V. SETH D.[8], born at Livermore, June 21, 1832.

VI. ELLEN ABIAH[8], born at Livermore, May 26, 1842.

*Delia King, wife of Reuel Washburn, was a descendant in the fifth generation of Philip King of Weymouth, who moved to Taunton (now Raynham) about 1680. The line is as follows:

(1) Philip King (died 1710) and Judith Whitman.

(2) John King (1675-1741) and Alice Dean.

(3) Benjamin King (1718-1803) and 1st Abiah Leonard; 2d Deliverance Eddy.

(4) Barzillai King (1766-1822) and 1st Lucinda Gilmore; 2d Nelly McCloud.

(4) Abiah King (1762-1842) and Israel[6] Washburn.

(5) Delia King (1801-1886) and Reuel[7] Washburn.

Hon. Horatio King of Washington, D. C. (1812-1897), was of this family, being a son of Samuel and grandson of Benjamin[3] and Abiah Leonard King.

FAMILY OF GANEM W. WASHBURN.

8. GANEM W. WASHBURN, oldest son of Reuel and Delia King Washburn, was born at Livermore, Oct. 29, 1823. He was graduated at Bowdoin College in 1845, studied law with his father and with his cousin, Gov. Israel Washburn, Jr., at Orono, Maine, was admitted to the bar in Oxford County, 1847, and went to Oshkosh, Wisconsin, where he settled and made a home.

He served in the Senate of Wisconsin, 1859 and 1860. He was County Judge, 1861-1864, and Judge of the Circuit Court from 1864 to 1879, when he resigned.

He married at Oshkosh, Wisconsin, Nov. 19, 1850, Sarah Perley Strickland, who was born at Livermore, Oct. 8, 1826.

Children of same: All born at Oshkosh, Wis.

I. CLARA ELIZABETH[9], born Oct. 5, 1851.

II. JOHN REUEL[9], born May 6, 1853.

III. MARY GERTRUDE[9], born Feb. 9, 1855.

IV. ALICE[9], born Sept. 12, 1860.

V. BENJAMIN[9], born Sept. 12, 1860. "Bennie" died Sept. 16, 1861.

9. CLARA ELIZABETH WASHBURN, daughter of Ganem W. Washburn, married at Oshkosh, Wisconsin, March 14, 1877, Charles Henry Morgan, who was born in Alleghany Co., New York, July 5, 1843.

Very early in the Civil War Mr. Morgan enlisted in the 1st Wisconsin Regt. of Volunteers and served through the entire

period of the war, attaining the rank of Captain. He was eighteen months in Southern prisons, escaping from Libby Prison by Capt. Rose's famous tunnel.

After the war he studied law and was graduated from the Law Department of the University of New York, and went to Lamar, Missouri.

He served in the State Legislature of Missouri and eight years in Congress.

Children of same:

I. MARY GERTRUDE[10], born at Washington, D. C., Dec. 27, 1877.
II. CHARLES HENRY[10], Jr., born at Lamar, Mo., Oct. 12, 1879. Died at Lamar, Mo., July 2, 1880.
III. FRANKLIN BENJAMIN[10], born at Lamar, Mo., Dec. 20, 1881.
IV. WASHBURN SWIFT[10], born at Lamar, Mo., Jan. 6, 1883.
V. CLARA ELIZABETH[10], born at Lamar, Mo., Sept. 25, 1885.
VI. ALBERT DYE[10], born at Lamar Sept. 25, 1889.
VII. FREDERIC ARTHUR[10], born at Lamar, Sept. 19, 1891.
VIII. CHARLES HENRY, Jr.[10], born at Lamar July 29, 1894.
IX. NATALIE[10], born at Lamar Nov. 9, 1897.

Capt. Morgan was again mustered into the service of the United States in the war with Spain, on May 18, 1898, at Jefferson Barracks, Mo., and was commissioned by Gov. Stephens, Lieut. Col. of the 5th Regt. of Missouri Volunteers.

Mary Gertrude Morgan graduated from the State Normal School at Oshkosh, Wisconsin, in 1897.

Frank B. Morgan graduated from Lamar High School in 1898, and entered the Missouri State University the same year.

9. John Reuel Washburn, son of Ganem W. Washburn, married at Oshkosh, Wis., Oct. 11, 1876, Harriet Anna Green, who was born at Keeseville, New York, Dec. 2, 1854.

Children of same: All born at Oshkosh.

I. Sarah Elizabeth[10], born May 7, 1878.
II. Laura Elsie[10], born April 2, 1880.
III. Ganem[10], born Sept. 18, 1884.
IV. John Earl[10], born June 17, 1895.

9. Mary Gertrude Washburn, daughter of Ganem W. Washburn, graduated at Oshkosh High School, 1873. She married at Oshkosh, Wisconsin, May 2, 1895, Lorenzo Dow Harmon, who was born at Hodgdon, Maine, Jan. 30, 1841. Mr. Harmon served in the Civil War as Captain of Co. B, 37th Regiment, Wisconsin Vol. Infantry. He was wounded several times but not seriously, and remained in the army till the close of the war.

Children of same: Born at Oshkosh.

I. Helen[10], born Feb. 8, 1896.
II. Ellis Cady[10], born Dec. 14, 1897. Died Sept. 3, 1898.

9. Alice Washburn, daughter of G. W. Washburn, graduated at Oshkosh High School and took a special course in elocution in Boston for three years, and has since taught elocution and other branches in the Oshkosh High School.

FAMILY OF ALONZO WASHBURN.

8. ALONZO WASHBURN, second son of Reuel[7] and Delia King Washburn, was born at Livermore June 3, 1826. He was educated at Livermore and at Gorham Seminary. He enlisted in the Civil war Dec. 31, 1863, and served in Co. L, 3d Regiment Wisconsin Cavalry to the end of the war. He was mustered out October, 1865, as Quartermaster Sergeant.

He married at Livermore, Maine, Apr. 10, 1850, Jane Coolidge Strickland, who was born at Livermore, Jan. 24, 1823.

Children of same:

I. JULIA MARIA[9], born at Oshkosh, Wis., March 23, 1852.
II. WILLIAM HENRY[9], born at Weyauwega, Wis., Feb. 14, 1854.
III. ANNIE WESTON[9], born at Oshkosh, Wis., Dec. 26, 1855.

9. JULIA MARIA WASHBURN, daughter of Alonzo[8], married at Milwaukee, Wis., Apr. 5, 1886, Allen R. Towle of Chicago. Mr. Towle was born at Portland, Me., Jan. 20, 1852.

Children of same: All born at Chicago.

I. EDSON FOSTER[10], born Feb. 3, 1887.
II. FLORENCE WASHBURN[10], born Dec. 9, 1888.
III. WILLIAM WASHBURN[10], born May 26, 1893. Died at Chicago, July 10, 1894.
IV. ATHALINE RICH[10], born Sept. 10, 1895.

9. WILLIAM HENRY WASHBURN, son of Alonzo[8], was graduated in medicine at Rush Medical College, Chicago, Feb.

1877. He is Professor in the Wisconsin College of Physicians and Surgeons, Milwaukee, and is also Secretary of the Faculty and Board of Directors of the same institution. He is Physician to the Presbyterian, St. Joseph's and Johnston Emergency Hospitals. His home is in Milwaukee, Wis.

He married at Ishpeming, Michigan, Oct. 1, 1878, Esther Willson, who was born at Sydenham, Ontario, March 6, 1851.

Children of same:

I. ROBERT GLENDENNING[10], born at Ishpeming, Mich., July 1, 1879.
II. WILLIAM HENRY, JR.,[10] born at Florence, Wis., Aug. 15. 1880. Died at Florence, Wis., Nov. 7, 1880.
III. BEATRICE WILLIAM[10], born at Florence, Wis., Apr. 4, 1882.
IV. GANEM[10], born at Milwaukee, Wis., May 2, 1885. Died at Milwaukee, Apr. 26, 1886.

Robert Glendenning Washburn is in the Wisconsin State University, class of 1900.

9. ANNIE WESTON WASHBURN, daughter of Alonzo[8] and Jane C. Washburn, married at Florence, Wisconsin, May 9, 1882, John Scott Willson, who was born at Goderich, Ontario, Sept. 30, 1853.

Children of same:

I. JANE WASHBURN[10], born at Florence, Wis., June 15, 1883. Died at Florence, Wis., June 16, 1883.
II. BENJAMIN WASHBURN[10], born at Milwaukee, Wis., March 30, 1886.
III. ESTHER[10], born at Ironwood, Michigan, Apr. 3, 1891. Their home is at Ironwood, Mich.

FAMILY OF SETH D. WASHBURN.

8. SETH D. WASHBURN, youngest son of Reuel and Delia King Washburn, was born at Livermore, June 21, 1832.

He was educated at the schools of Livermore and the Academies of Farmington and Bloomfield. He studied law and was admitted to the Androscoggin Bar in 1861.

He married at Livermore March 8, 1871, Julia Constantia Chase, a descendant as well as himself from John Washburn of Duxbury. She was born at Turner, Dec. 10, 1840. Their home is at North Livermore, Maine.

NOTE.—Washburn Ancestors of Mrs. Julia Chase Washburn. JOHN[1], JOHN[2], JOSEPH[3] (?), BENJAMIN[4].

5. BENJAMIN, son of Benjamin[4], married Martha Kingman, 1729, and died at Bridgewater, 1740.

6. BENJAMIN, son of Benjamin[5], born 1735, married Desire Sears of Halifax, 1762, and died at Bridgewater, 1796.

7. MARY, daughter of Benjamin[6] and Desire Sears Washburn, was born at Bridgewater, Mass., June 29, 1780. She married at Bridgewater Nov. 30, 1801, Barzillai Latham, a descendant in the fifth generation of Robert Latham, who married Susanna Winslow, daughter of John Winslow and MARY CHILTON, and niece of Gov. Edward Winslow. Mary Washburn Latham died at Buckfield, Me., Aug. 19, 1854.

8. REBECCA DEAN LATHAM, daughter of Barzillai and Mary Washburn Latham, was born at Buckfield, Me., Jan. 23, 1805. She married at Buckfield, June 8, 1831, Job Chase, who was born at Buckfield, June 28, 1806, and died at Livermore, May 27, 1891.

Rebecca Latham Chase died at Livermore, Dec. 15, 1884.

Children of Job and Rebecca Latham Chase:

I. MARY LATHAM³, born at Sangerville, Me., Apr. 5, 1832. Married H. M. Bearce. Died at Boston, June 22, 1882.

II. GEORGE FRANKLIN⁹, born at Sangerville, Me., Nov. 24, 1834. Died at Statesville, N. C., Oct. 18, 1898.

III. JULIA CONSTANTIA, born at Turner, Me., Dec. 10, 1840.

FAMILY OF ELLEN WASHBURN SMITH.

8. ELLEN ABIAH WASHBURN, daughter of Reuel[7] and Delia King Washburn, was born at Livermore, May 26, 1842.

She married at Livermore on the Golden-wedding day of her parents, Oct. 19, 1870, Roscoe Smith, M. D.

Dr. Smith was born at Peru, Maine, Nov. 13, 1839. He attended Maine State Seminary (now Bates College) 1858-1863. He was at Bates College after the war, '65-67, at Maine Medical School, Brunswick, 1868-1869, and was graduated at Harvard Medical School in 1870.

In the Civil War he enlisted in Co. I, 3d Maine Vols. in 1863. and served till 1865. He was wounded at Spotsylvania; after which he was connected with the surgical department of the hospital.

He represented the town of Turner in the State Legislature in 1891.

Child of same:

REUEL WASHBURN[9], born at Turner, Me., Sept. 19, 1875. He was graduated at Bowdoin College in 1897 and entered the Law School of Harvard University in 1898.

FAMILY OF ELI KING WASHBURN.

7. ELI KING WASHBURN, youngest son of Israel⁶ and Abiah King Washburn, was born at Raynham, Mass., July 22. 1802.

He spent his life on the old Washburn homestead at Raynham. He represented his town in the Legislature of Massachusetts and was an ardent temperance man and abolitionist.

He married Dec. 25, 1825, Nancy Dean Norton, who was born at Mansfield, Mass., Aug. 28, 1806.

He died at Raynham, July 28, 1852, aged 50.

She died at Taunton, Mass., May 26, 1873, aged 66.

Children of same: All born at Raynham.

I. THOMAS⁸, born Jan. 6, 1827. Died at Raynham July 8, 1870.

II. EMILY⁸, born Apr. 28, 1828. Died at Mansfield, Mass., Aug. 11, 1896.

III. NATHAN⁸, born Dec. 29, 1829.

IV. MARY⁸, born Oct. 27, 1832. Died at Raynham, Nov. 4, 1855.

V. LUCY⁸, born Oct. 8, 1834. Died at Raynham, Nov. 5, 1855.

VI. LAURA⁸, born Aug. 28, 1836. Died at Brockton, Mass., May 21, 1887.

VII. CAMILLA⁸, born March 17, 1838. Died at Raynham, Nov 2, 1855.

Family of Eli King Washburn

VIII. ARTHUR[8], born Apr. 26, 1840. Died at Brockton, Mass., Aug. 24, 1892.

IX. MIRIAM[8], born Feb. 5, 1842. Died at Mansfield, Mass., Dec. 30, 1855.

X. JANE[8], born March 22, 1844. Died at Raynham Oct. 30, 1855.

XI. JULIET[8], born Apr. 5, 1846.

XII. MARTHA[8], born Sept. 13, 1851. Died at Raynham Sept. 14, 1854.

NOTE.—The five deaths in this family in 1855 were from typhoid fever.

8. THOMAS WASHBURN, son of Eli King Washburn, married at Taunton, Mass., Nov. 25, 1866, Mary Bowers Hall, who was born at Taunton, Mass., Jan. 12, 1834.

Thomas Washburn went to California in 1849 and remained there till 1862, making one trip home in the time.

He died at Raynham on the old Washburn homestead July 8, 1870.

Child of same:

9. HARRY THOMAS WASHBURN, born at Raynham Nov. 24, 1868. He still owns (1898) the old Washburn home in Raynham where his father built a new house. The old house, in which Israel[7] and Reuel[7] were born, is still standing, but no longer used as a dwelling. (See cut, page 34.)

Harry T. married at Taunton, Nov. 30, 1897, Florence Westcoat, who was born at Taunton, Mass., Nov. 1, 1870.

Their home is at Taunton.

8. EMILY WASHBURN, daughter of Eli K.[7] Washburn, married Lloyd E. Allen March 31, 1854. She died at Mansfield, Mass., Aug. 11, 1896.

8. LAURA WASHBURN, daughter of Eli King[7] Washburn, married Charles F. Field Jan. 1, 1868. She died at Brockton, Mass., May 21, 1887.

Children of same: All born at Brockton, Mass.
I. CHARLES WASHBURN[9], born 1868.
II. ALBERT D.[9], born Sept. 5, 1869.
III. EUSTACE[9], born Sept. 1, 1871.
IV. LAURA J.[9], born Feb. 17, 1873.
V. HELEN M.[9], born Dec. 7, 1875.

9. EUSTACE FIELD, son of Charles F. and Laura Washburn[8] Field, married at Brockton, Mass., 1894, Harriet M. Petty.

Children of same: Born at Brockton.
I. MILDRED AUGUSTA[10], born July 8, 1895.
II. RUTH ELIZABETH[10], born Nov. 8, 1896.

9. LAURA J. FIELD, daughter of Charles F. and Laura Washburn[8] Field, married at Brockton September, 1898, Frank Makepeace of Brockton.

8. ARTHUR WASHBURN, son of Eli King[7] Washburn, married, 1st, Rebecca Gifford, April 27, 1875, and 2d, Emma Cunningham, May 25, 1886. He died at Brockton, Mass., Aug. 24, 1892.

8. JULIET WASHBURN, daughter of Eli King[7] Washburn,

married, 1st, Charles F. Ivers, 1873, and 2d, Abel S. Amerzeen, July 4, 1884.

Children of 1st marriage:

I. AMY LEONARD[9], born at Taunton, Mass., Apr. 5, 1875.
II. LUCY WASHBURN[9], born at Taunton, Mass., Dec. 15, 1877.

Child of 2d marriage:

III. ADA MARIA[9], born at Brockton, Mass., Apr. 15, 1886.

Changing but one word, a quotation from Judge Ezekiel Whitman in his memoir of John Whitman, seems a fitting close to this book.

"The posterity of John 'WASHBURN' will seldom find occasion to blush upon looking back upon the past lives of those from whom they have derived their origin. Fortunate indeed may the generations now in being esteem themselves, if they can be sure to bequeath to their posterity an equal source of felicitation."

ADDITIONS AND CORRECTIONS.

Page 26—
    IV. Samuel³, born 1651; married Deborah Packard.

Page 50—
    Israel Henry⁹ Washburn was born 1843.

Page 51—
    11. Emily Washburn, daughter of Israel Henry, Jr¹⁰. and Virginia Sanborn Washburn, was born at Portsmouth, N. H. Feb. 7, 1899.

Page 60—
    Adèle Bertrand¹⁰ Washburn died 1884.

Page 66—
    9. Elizabeth C. Stephenson died at Brookline, Mass., Feb. 10, 1899.

Page 88—
    Ganem W⁹. Washburn was born Oct. 29.

INDEX.

	PAGE
Allen, Emily Washburn, family of	98
Amerzeen, Juliet Washburn, family of	99
Arms of Washburn family	17
Baldwin, Mary Washburn, family of	75
Benjamin, Martha	43
Bishop, Susan Washburne, family of	61
Botkine, Frances Payson, family of	65
Brown, Robina Napier	50
Buffum, Mary Washburn, family of	72
Butler, Ellen Hamlin, poem of	37
Benjamin Genealogy	46
Buise, Lula Grace	60
Carkiner, Gertrude Emily	73
Chase, Julia Constantia	94
Cleaveland, Sallie Catherine	68
Clarke, Annie M	60
English Notes of the Washburn Family	5
Evesham branch of the Washburn Family	19
Eddy, Deliverance	34
Field, Laura Washburn, family of	98
Fobes, Leah	30
Forbes, Rev. Perez, D. D. (A "call")	30
Foster, Olive Leonard, family of	81
Fowler, Marie Washburne, family of	61
Garr, Jeannette	63
Green, Harriett Anna	90
Harding, Elizabeth Pope	53
Hand, Eliza E	67
Howell, Hester Washburn, family of	69
Harmon, Mary Washburn, family of	90
Hall, Mary Bowers	97
Holmes, Caroline Washburn, family of	77
Ivers, Charles F	99
Jackson, Arabella V	51
Kellogg, Katherine Washburn, family of	71

King, Abiah.. 33
King, Delia.. 87
Kelsey, Jeannette Washburn, family of........................ 63
Le Ghait, Jeannette Payson, family of........................ 65
Leonard, Molly Washburn, family of........................... 78
Library, Washburn Memorial................................... 57
Lucas, Martha Stephenson, family of.......................... 67
Manor-House at Wicheniord.................................... 9
Massasoit.. 24
Mitchell, Elizabeth.. 26
Moore, Sarah Ann... 52
Muzzy, Elizabeth Little...................................... 74
Morgan, Clara Washburn, family of............................ 88
Norlands, The.. 36
Norton, Nancy Dean... 96
Poems of Thomas Washburn, D. D............................... 14
Packard, Deborah... 28
Payson, Fanny Washburn, family of............................ 64
Revolutionary Record of Israel Washburn[5]................... 30
Revolutionary Record of Israel Washburn[6]................... 34
Reade, Addie Brown... 71
Sanborn, Virginia.. 51
Savier, Mary Louise.. 53
Savier, Florence Agnes....................................... 75
Severance, Luther.. 54
Sumner, Waitstill.. 29
Stark, Ada Buffum, family of................................. 73
Smith, Margaret V.. 72
Smith, Ellen Washburn, family of............................. 95
Stephenson, Martha Washburn, family of....................... 66
Strickland, Sarah P.. 88
Strickland, Jane C... 91
Thompson, Lorette May.. 70
Towle, Julia Washburn, family of............................. 91
Washbournes of England....................................... 5
Washburn, John[1] of Evesham................................. 24-25
Washburn, John[2].. 20
Washburn, Philip[2].. 25
Washburn, Samuel[3].. 28
Washburn, Emory.. 27
Washburn, Israel[1].. 29
Washburn, Israel[2].. 34

Washburn, Israel[6]... 34
Washburn, Nehemiah[6], and family................................. 33
Washburn, Seth[6], and family... 33
Washburn, Oliver[6], and family....................................... 33
Washburn, Israel[7]—1784-1876....................................... 39
Washburn, Israel[7], children of....................................... 47
Washburn, Israel[8], Jr., family of.................................... 48
Washburn, Israel Henry[9], family of................................ 50
Washburn, Israel Henry[10], Jr., family of......................... 51
Washburn, Algernon Sidney[8], family of.......................... 52
Washburn, John[9], family of.. 53
Washburn, Charles Robert[9], family of............................ 53
Washburne, Elihu Benjamin[8], family of.......................... 54
Washburne, Hempstead[7], family of................................ 59
Washburne, William Pitt[9], family of............................... 60
Washburn, Cadwallader Colden[8], family of..................... 62
Washburn, Charles Ames[8], family of.............................. 68
Washburn, Samuel Benjamin[8], family of......................... 70
Washburn, Samuel Benjamin[9], Jr., family of.................... 71
Washburn, William Drew[8], family of............................... 74
Washburn, William Drew[9], Jr., family of.......................... 75
Washburn, Benjamin[7], family of.................................... 84
Washburn, Reuel[7], family of... 85
Washburn, Ganem W.[8], family of.................................. 88
Washburn, John Reuel[9], family of.................................. 90
Washburn, Alonzo[8], family of....................................... 91
Washburn, William Henry[9], family of.............................. 91
Washburn, Seth D.[8], family of....................................... 93
Washburn, Eli King[7], family of...................................... 96
Washburn, Thomas[8], family of...................................... 97
Washburn, Harry Thomas[9], family of.............................. 97
Washburn, Arthur[9], family of.. 98
Washburn, Great and Little... 5
Washburn tombs in England... 11
Webster, Mary Maud... 49
Westcoat, Florence... 97
Wichenford Court, England... 9
Wichenford Church, England... 11
Willson, Annie Washburn, family of.................................. 92
Willson, Esther... 92